THE IMAGE THEY SEE

The Ability to Be Who I Am

Paul R. Becker

authorHOUSE®

AuthorHouse™
1663 Liberty Drive
Bloomington, IN 47403
www.authorhouse.com
Phone: 1 (800) 839-8640

Published by AuthorHouse 09/06/2018

ISBN: 978-1-5462-5859-9 (sc)
ISBN: 978-1-5462-5857-5 (hc)
ISBN: 978-1-5462-5858-2 (e)

Library of Congress Control Number: 2018910359

Print information available on the last page.

We struggle to simply be accepted in our world. Our community has come a long way but there are many more bridges to cross. Working together in our communities and within our own families will make a difference some-day.

The ability to celebrate a unity without prejudice or fear of not being accepted is hard to imagine.

Let us unite together and create a world that is not filled with hate. We need not judge others as no one is exempt from feeling left out.

All of us need to feel accepted and not be defined by the judgement of others.

We own our lives and how we live it paves the path to invite others on our journey.

Live by the true definition of **Diversity**.

Introduction

Each morning I wake up and begin the process to start my day. It's a new day and as I wipe the sleep from my eyes I begin to feel refreshed. Most mornings I awake before the alarm and usually listen for the coffee maker to start brewing. I lay still and listen to the sounds of the morning. The birds begin to sing outside the window and a car passes by the house every morning as the driver tosses newspapers out the window onto our driveways.

I start down the stairs and switch on lights trying to keep quiet so I don't disturb Kyle and Madison. Pour my coffee and prepare Madison's breakfast (our dog). After placing her plate on the floor I sit down and turn the TV on to our local news channel. With a deep breath I take my first sip of coffee and start thinking of the day ahead.

Most mornings I check my email. Of course most are advertisements and offers to buy new windows. I don't remember signing up to get window deals but some day we may need them.

Before my second sip of coffee I log onto Facebook and post my morning message and picture. Usually a simple salutation; *Good Morning. Have a great day.*

After Madison wakes up and eats its usually time for our morning walk. One of us grabs a flashlight and the other hooks the leash to Madison's collar. We welcome the morning sun as we stroll through the neighborhood. It's quiet and most mornings the homes are dark. It's a peaceful time. When we get back to the house I finish my coffee and hit the shower. Now time to get ready for work.

When I come back downstairs I eat breakfast, always yogurt, banana and orange juice. Guess I am pretty simple. Afterwards I brush my teeth and off to work. My drive is easy and usually takes me twenty minutes. I Typically park in the same garage and most days I get my same spot in the garage on the second floor. Talk about routine. The parking garage is very close to the building I work in.

As I enter the front door I take on a different persona.

Mentally I prepare to greet anyone who may see me as a *label*.

Nowhere in my thought process is fear of who I am. I don't worry how people will perceive me because *I am Who I Am*.

I set out to make a difference and influence others as I manage my staff to succeed. It's my job to make sure they grow in their career and become the person they have set out to be. I'm not doing my job if they fail. Because if they fail, I do too.

Chapter 1

The Recipe

Just like Aunt Collette's famous lasagna, which is full of ingredient's that no one can duplicate, so are the characteristics we all have. Others have tried to duplicate her Lasagna but fall short on the exact ingredients. Although she wrote it down on index cards the end result would differ depending on who makes it. Maybe it requires just the right glass of wine.

No one has the recipe to bring the right people together. There is no written index card which describes what measurement of characteristics is appropriate. That's life. But as we come together and mix, it's more important to combine together and not judge the unique flavors that result from our recipe.

It does not matter what background you come from or the sexual orientation you accept; it's about existing together without hatred towards one another. No one should be judged.

We should be able to walk down the street, heads held high and know the world is ours.

The recipe for success is about knowing yourself and having confidence that others see you for the outstanding work you do. Never should we alter the recipe because of fear that others may not accept you.

Aunt Collette's recipe would have different flavors depending on who is making it. Surely would be different if Kathleen, Carol, Patty or Debbie chose to leave something out or add a spice they like better. It's what is best for them. They don't ask anyone for an opinion because it does not matter.

Our characteristics are not a unit of measure; ½ teaspoon of straight with a ¼ teaspoon of feminine. Each of us has been pre-measured with an expiration date and a blend of ingredients that make us who we are today. We aspire to exceed our shelf life and make sure that within that time our existence is noticed like the new product displayed on the grocery store shelf.

The bottom line is it all comes together and blends. That is what makes us special.

In any recipe we tend to read the labels so we can identify all the ingredients. Labels need to be precise and specifically identify each component of the package or can. We cannot change or switch labels as it was packaged that way from the time of production. Sound familiar?

I realize comparing life to a recipe is far-fetched. But is it really? It's interesting to compare so many simple things we see and do every day to how we see and interact with each other.

Our World is a mixture of so many personalities, faces and ethnic backgrounds. From the beginning of time and the moment the Pilgrims set foot in America we began mixing together to form a family. Any recipe is prone to alterations and life is no different.

Chapter 2

Labels

At one point we have labelled someone we know or a person we meet for the first time. Human nature takes over and we tend to see people for not who they are not, but for the people we think they are. There are times we can read a person and get a feel for their personality. Usually the one loud person in a group who has no respect for anyone around them, does not necessarily mean they are a bad person. The quiet girl or boy sitting in the corner is not 'strange', they choose to be less noticed. That crazy neighbor who sets dolls outside in her garden may not be the first person we would invite to dinner, but may be a person we should at least take a moment to say hello.

Our label should not be from speculation or rumors of who they think we are. Those labels have been a part of our society for a long time. When we are out with friends of the same sex the whisper from across the room is deafening. Of course a table full of men cannot just be; "a table full of men". Why is that? However, a table full of woman simple is; "a table full of woman". It's very interesting how we view those scenarios.

It's funny how we judge our environment differently. Most times a single woman at the office, in a social environment usually is identified as just not finding the right guy yet. The single man usually over 30 is immediately tagged with a label. Oh, and if he is well dressed that will certainly seal the deal. Why is that?

Usually in our working environments people ask about your personal life as topic of conversation and try to get to know you. Those conversations most times lead to asking about your family. Unfortunately, we are placed in an uncomfortable position because the person asking those questions typically is someone who may not accept our true answer. In my new skin I tend to hold the truth back until I am more familiar with my environment. Why is it most people are not afraid to say; "I have a wife, a husband, boyfriend and/or girlfriend".

I should not have to think of a reaction when I state I have a Partner. Although my family structure may not meet the standard mold, it's what works for us. My label should be that I have a solid relationship and I am a professional person who has worked hard at life. Certainly not up for renegotiation.

In many institutions our relationship is acceptable, even to the point of most business now recognize us as a couple. We can now marry too. But in some families the recognition of us being a couple tends to be the unspoken reality. If I chose to marry my partner, there should never be hesitation of who I would invite to witness the ceremony. Of course I'm not wearing the flowing white gown and walking down the aisle, but I would like the acceptance of the person I love every day until death do us part.

When we moved into our previous neighborhood there was hesitation as to how we would be accepted. During the house search there was never a moment I thought it would make a difference. However, during the buying process one neighbor began to petition that we don't buy the house. Certainly that was greeted with much hesitation of moving forward with buying. But we continued and moved on. I guess you get a sense of your future neighbors as you drive thru. After moving in neighbors greeted us and accepted us as neighbors, not a label of the gay couple next door. Of course we would bring a sense of style to the neighborhood.

That's not a bad label to have.

It was interesting over the years to be accepted by who we are and not by our sexual orientation. Funny part is that same person who petitioned us from moving into the neighborhood allowed her son to play basketball on our driveway. So what really was her issue? I think it was her own insecurities.

They say "don't judge a book by its cover" and I strongly believe that. Sometime we are so quick to make assumptions about others and really don't know them. It should never matter what someone believes in. We like people because they add value to our lives. There is a reason why we have welcomed these individuals into our inner circle.

Chapter 3

It's All in The Greeting

In certain situation's the simple act of an introduction can be uncomfortable for many. There are no set rules but having common sense seems to be a good approach. Understanding who you are introducing is important too. It's not about making someone feel ashamed about who they are or the person in their lives.

I remember the first time Kyle and I began living together. Although it was not awkward to us it was to others.

Most times we were introduced as "roommates" or "friends." When family came to our home it was always "Paul's room" or "Kyle's room" and there was always the question of "who's house is this?"

That is one of many challenges we face. We have come a long way but not there yet.

We should never have to hide behind closed doors or feel uncomfortable in our own homes.

The best introduction I ever had was Kyle's father. We were attending his Grandmother's milestone birthday and sitting in a room filled with family and friends. Lum was asked to speak and give a toast to his mother. Each of his siblings introduced their family in the fire hall. So as Lum started to introduce his son Kevin and then Kyle it came to me. There was a hesitation and I'm sure to Lum it seemed like hours, but the next words he spoke were special. I was introduced as Barb and Lum's third son Paul who is very special to their family. Wow!

That was not easy but it was met with no remorse or regret, although at some tables the conversation led to a discussion of our relationship. It does not matter how we are defined as long as we are accepted.

When we enter a conference room for a meeting and go around the room to introduce ourselves we should never worry about who we are, because that should never matter. Our Human Resource departments tell us that we cannot discriminate against anyone and that is true. So why is it so different on the outside?

In social situations most people talk about their children or spouse. For many years I used the title of divorced, just to hide behind who I truly was, mostly because people would not accept the truth. In many ways it was unfair.

The definition of relationship is; *the way in which two or more concepts, objects, or people are connected, or the state of being connected.*

When I think about a connection my mind relates that to our souls. We all strive for a soul mate when we begin dating and seeking our partner for life.

The next time you are in any social situation think about your introductions when introducing your family, friends and neighbors. It's okay to ask someone how they would like to be introduced. Obviously it is much more comfortable for everyone and you are not offending anyone. Honesty is the best policy. In these situation's it helps to create an environment that is more comfortable.

Now in my mid 50's I am comfortable introducing my partner as just that, I don't feel the need to sugar coat my relationship.

Chapter 4

Born This Way

I could never understand how the Institution that taught me to Sit, Stand and Kneel would turn their back and say I don't belong. The same Institution that welcomed me in my mother's arms the day I was Baptized. Truth be told I was "Born This Way."

When we accept the sacraments through our Catholic upbringing there is never a moment we are judge or labeled. At no point is there any doubt this Institution we devote our lives to would ever turn its back. But they do. Not just because *"I Am Who I Am."*

There are rules that we are programmed to believe and follow, and certainly there is not much room for deviation. It's about respect and accepting all who are different and don't fit the mold.

Who would know at the time of Baptism that a man or woman would get married and divorce?

In my situation I was married and divorced and then accepted the fact of being in a solid relationship that the Church disapproves.

So whether I choose to live my life outside the rules should be no different than anyone else. We were all welcomed into the Church and given the names we would be known by until death. My God is your God too.

This year we decided to attend a Catholic service for Christmas. With much hesitation I chose the Church and we went to the 10am Christmas Day service. Walking into the building I could honestly feel the tension build in me. As the service started I began listening to the parishioners around me recite the words we all group up on with through Sit, Stand and Kneel. At one point in the service we are asked to reach out and share the sign of peace. Everyone greets the people beside them with a handshake and simple words of "peace be with you."

Sitting in front of us are neighbors who we have become friends with since moving into our home. When Larry turned around to shake my hand his words were special and should have been shouted from the pulpit. Larry said, "you know you are welcome here any time." I was blown away by that simple phrase and will remember that forever.

Does our Church really listen?

It should not matter where or when I choose to worship or say a prayer. My voice is heard the same as anyone else. People need to be accepted no matter what. Truth be told, if I was giving a donation to the institution I was raised with I would bet my check is cashed and not labeled 'return to sender.' Nor am I coded in the "books" as 'not welcomed.'

These situations are never easy and certainly people don't feel it should be talked about. We need to have a voice and let it be heard.

For many years growing up and finding my true self I spent countless hours rehearsing in my head my coming out speech. I thought about the pros and cons and who would be accepting of me. It should never be this hard for anyone, but for some those challenges weigh heavy on their shoulders.

Thinking back, I can remember my first conversation with my mom. We were actually on vacation at a friend's B&B in Delaware. It was early in the morning and Mom and I were sitting on the front porch having our coffee. My hands were sweating and I had a huge lump in my throat. It was after my divorce and I finally knew 'me.' I took a sip of coffee and looked at my mom and said, "I have something to tell you". In her gentle voice she met my glance and simply said, "we love you". I did not get the point but proceeded to give the speech I rehearsed the night before. I finally said the words; "Mom, I am gay." She wiped a tear and gave me a hug and said; "you're our son and we want you to be happy." That was all the reassurance I needed. We continued talking and it made me proud to share my journey with my mom. It was a special time that we were able to bond and spend time and mother and son. It's those moments we cherish for a lifetime.

If only it was this easy for everyone. So many young people struggle and many men who come out later in life are ashamed. I think we all regress and try to suppress our feelings. I remember thinking these feelings would go away. Now I understand why. We have only now been more accepted in our communities as in the past.

It was easier with my dad. Well I honestly say he fell right into the conversation. Dad was out shopping around town and came back to the B&B with a flag. He wanted to hang the flag outside their home in Pittsburgh. As he described his purchase we anticipated what was going to pull out of the bag. Of course his enthusiasm was overwhelming and finally my mom said; "Bob, what did you buy?"

As he pulled the flag out of the plastic bag I began to chuckle and eventually the other guests staying at the B&B began to laugh. The flag my Dad bought to hang on their home in Pittsburgh was the Rainbow Flag which represents the Gay Community. It was touching to see the excitement on his face but the reality of it was something we surely needed to discuss. So Mom and I had our talk with dad and it was much easier than I would ever imagine. Dad wanted to make sure I was happy and he was proud that I had a conversation with he and mom. Well, now the flag.

My Dad was working at the Church performing his Deacon responsibilities so I felt maybe we needed to exchange the flag for something less 'OUT.' Mom, Dad and I walked to the store and found something more suitable for a Deacon in the Catholic Church.

Honestly, looking back I wish he would have kept that flag and made a statement. It would have symbolized his being proud and accepting of his son. Although with everything happening in the Church I guess it was for the best.

Chapter 5

Domestic Partner

The first time I chose to include my partner as an emergency contact at work was a big step. I remember thinking that my adding him under the title of 'Domestic Partner' would 'Out' me at work. Of course it did not and I don't know why I was nervous.

One of our good friends Chas was working as an Electrician and installing lighting fixtures in the mid-west. He was in an accident which required him to be hospitalized and the outlook was not good. Chas chose to use a fake name as his emergency contact but the phone number was his partner's. When the company called his partner they were looking for "Lisa", and of course there was no "Lisa" on the other end. It was sad because Chas needed to know his family was notified.

After many attempts to reach "Lisa" the company got in touch with his parents and finally after many calls to "Lisa" the connections were made and everyone was on the same page. There was an accident, Chas was hurt and trips to the mid-west were made. However, these two families knew nothing about each other, until they finally came together at the Hospital. "Lisa" was introduced as Rob and Chas' family immediately put the pieces together. For many years the reality of this relationship was hidden. Only because Chas' family would not have been accepting.

It's sad to think that we hide behind the truth because others don't accept us. The dynamic of family comes in many forms and definitions of *Domestic Partner* has additional meanings.

Unfortunately, Chas passed away after fighting to survive his accident. I don't know if these two families remain in contact but at least finally in his passing Chas can be at rest with the truth of his relationship.

I think there are many people in similar situations and hide behind their own reality. It's difficult to have those conversations but lifting the weight off your shoulders is a huge relief. For many years I struggled with the truth and finally found the right time to have a talk.

I am proud every year to check that box on my emergency contact page and proud that I can be comfortable to share my 'domestic partner' with my company.

I remember the first time I was introduced to a gay couple and they referred to each other as "my lover". It was not the best title and I could never figure out what the best one would be. Then I would hear; "my boyfriend", "my partner" and now we are introduced as a "husband" if married. I guess having multiple titles and options is not so bad.

Chapter 6

When I knew

In many situations and conversation's, I am always asked the question of "When did you know?" I sometimes laugh to myself at that question because I think it should be re-worded. That question should spark opposing questions to whomever is curious enough to inquire.

The simplest answer is; *The moment I was conceived.*

However, the opposing question should be; *When did I recognize my true inner feelings?*

When I reflect back to my earlier years I try to find the answer to these questions. It's not easy. I don't honestly think when I was young I would have ever been able to distinguish my true feelings or understand my sexuality enough to be sure. I can honestly say it was harder back then because we were not exposed to the lifestyles that so many don't want us to be.

Fifty plus years ago we did not have TV shows like Wil & Grace for so many people who have become advocates to our community. We repressed the feelings because our religion forbade it and our families did not understand.

So when did I know?

If I dig deep into my soul, I can say my first feelings were in my early teen years. So many changes were happening in my body and my mind was racing to understand the feelings I was trying to push away.

Growing up there were celebrities, athletes and classmates that I recognized as being handsome. I guess at those times maybe I just figured it was a normal part of growing up. There were always those department store catalogs with the handsome models showing off the latest fashions. Thinking back, I remember my friends always talking about the Sears Catalog and looking at the woman's lingerie section. That catalog was a big hit when the Christmas edition came out.

It was unfortunate but I pushed back any emotions that were leading me towards a life of sin, or at least I thought that was my destiny.

I'm sure I was not alone and I would bet many young men suppress these feelings, it's sad because it takes a toll on you emotionally. To me this was the point of acceptance or take a road which would eventually lead towards many sleepless nights of guilt.

Guilt should be the emotion when we do something that is not ethical or we personally hurt someone we love. It should not be a word that defines who I am.

So the next time you ask someone the question of "when did you know?" think of the emotion behind those four words. Most of us struggle to understand why we were born this way and why we continue to fight for a place in our World. It should not be this hard.

Bottom line is; *I am Paul I am me, your approval isn't needed.*

When we were young we sought approval by our parents for many things we thought was best. The first time we wanted to experiment with a new hairstyle, the first time we got our ear (s) pierced and of course approval for the college we wanted to attend.

But when we become adults the responsibility of our actions we own whether right or wrong. Of course we think of the consequences of our decisions and the anticipation of an outcome can be overwhelming. It's the unknown which we fear.

Coming to terms with who you are is no different. We fear what others will think and the only thing we want is to be accepted no matter the outcome. Often times you read and hear of families turning their backs on family who choose to express their sexuality. How sad. Actually it's is most sad for the family members who walk away, they will never see the great person you become.

Chapter 7

Break The Rules

No matter what we do there are always rules associated with how we achieve an end result. If we stick to the rules and play the game, we tend to be rewarded for our efforts.

I remember playing the game of Life as a kid. We would sit around the dining room table and my sister, Mom and Dad would play. Dad was always the Banker, of course it suited him since he was an Auditor in real life.

We began by picking our pegs, blue for boys and pink for girls. Then we pushed those pegs into our cars and waited for Dad to set up our bank accounts. Each player started with $10,000.00, seemed like a lot back then. These days that won't buy you a college education.

I just remember those plastic cars were not very sporty. Just a square plastic care with no options. Certainly had to use your imagination.

The first spin of the wheel determined your career path, if only it was that easy. That first spin decided if you would go to College or jump into a job. The career path guaranteed that you would be closer to earning an income and the object of this game is to finish with the most money. Was not a hard decision to figure out which way I wanted to go.

As you pass across the board you get married, had children and eventually begin the task of paying the Banker back. Sounds familiar right? Although you collect money as you progress along the board, there seems to be that unexpected expense. We all know that feeling.

So the rules of life require you to marry and have children, only because the rules of the game are set. The path is outlined and the winner takes all. The key is to save enough money for retirement and maybe join the Millionaire Circle. In the end the family who retires with the largest bank account win the game of life.

The creators of the game had a goal in mind when the game was invented. As they created each step across the board there was much discussion on how the players would interact with the rules. Paydays were decided and with each spin of the wheel we move closer to the end.

No different in our real lives. Our instructions were clear, we have goals and in the end we strive to be winners. In our human lives we want success and happiness and someone to care for us until we die.

So why not change the rules and insert new ones as long as the end result is the same? Who I choose to be in my 'car of life' is my own, because it's 'my rule'. Maybe the Millionaire Circle is not my ultimate end, but happiness is so how I get there is up to me.

In any relationship the rules need to be agreed to and certainly it's okay to be different. No one hands us a formal set of rules and asks for a signature holding us to a planned outcome. It's ours to change and as long as there is commitment to work towards the Millionaire Circle then so be it.

Be open minded, get creative, be passionate on your outcome. Don't disrespect one another or hurt the other person in your 'car of life'. Celebrate your success!

It's your game of life, play it well.

Chapter 8

Diversity

The word Diversity is defined as; *the condition of having or being composed of differing elements : the inclusion of different types of people (such as people of different races or cultures) in a group or organization* : an instance of being composed of differing elements or qualities : an instance of being diverse .

If you take the time to understand the words that describe this one word it can set the tone for so many things. As human beings we were created to be different. We are not carbon copies of another person, nor should we live our lives to satisfy a definition that someone has categorized us into.

So many companies express the importance of Diversity and educate their employees on the many aspects of this word. It's not just about our nationalities, color of our skin or the ratios of employees on our teams. We are educated to treat everyone with respect.

In any community or walk of life we all strive for respect and to be accepted. It should not matter if you have $1 or $10 million in your banking account, because at the end of the day we were all brought into this world the same. For anyone who thinks otherwise I would challenge that they too were met with similar challenges growing up. It's the life choices we make that leads to our success or failures.

We are presented with choices and certainly I have made the wrong ones along the way which has helped me grow into the person I am today.

When I was young and started to learn of other cultures and religions I can remember hearing about how others lived and prayed. It was hard at first to understand the scope of what I was be taught because at that time I only knew what I knew, and that was what my family, friends and school taught me.

Who knew at a young age I was learning the true definition of Diversity.

I can remember the first time I was introduced to a Jewish family and went to Temple for their service and participated in a Passover meal and celebration. The service and meal were explained in full detail and I learned so many fascinating stories about this religion. It was cool.

Our holiday celebrations, no matter which religion we believe are different too. We create our own traditions and they become an important part of our family history.

These are all examples of Diversity and become acceptable by all walks of life. We don't judge or influence traditions, we simply "accept". Which is exactly what we all wish for over time.

So if you really search back in your upbringing and understand the teachings as a young person we have been programmed to accept. It does not matter which form it comes in or whom it affects, it's what we do.

What changes then? The definition changes over time because we allow others to influence us to believe the word holds another meaning. When most people hear "diversity" it's associated with the Gay Community. It provokes conversation and establishes a boundary as to who is accepted. I see "diversity" as an ever evolving word which will always continue to define our world.

Chapter 9

Eye Contact

My Grandmother always taught me that you judge a person by looking in their eyes, it's the portal to the soul. Of course the other person has to reciprocate. The eyes tell all! But there are so many who cannot make eye contact whether it is a first introduction or a conversation between friends. Some people have a hard time with that, although it truly is a matter of trust.

Occasionally you meet a person who tends to look beyond you or glances towards the ceiling. Some choose to look at the floor and maybe concentrate on the scenery at your back. It's difficult to determine what reception you'll get but you can certainly make the best of any of these examples.

Our eyes take in so much information throughout our lives and they record events which feeds our brain and stores that moment forever. It's like going to a movie and hitting rewind, pause and play for a lifetime.

Trust is an important aspect of eye contact too. Immediately you can identify who is listening and if you can divulge a secret knowing it won't be shared with others. You can never know that for sure but we all have tried and have been burned.

The reason our eyes feed the soul is because of what they take in every day. If we cannot see, our minds take over and the image we physically cannot take in is substituted by a description that is usually more vivid.

Sometimes images become a perception that dictates our impressions of others. We tend to get a visual of others which leads us to make judgements.

My favorite artist is Margaret Keane who paints the Big Eye prints. Her paintings are usually of people, young, old and on occasion a dog or cat. In all her paintings the image she paints has larger than normal eyes. The eyes tell her story and you tend to be drawn in. Mostly they appear sad but she clearly defines that the eyes are leading you to her soul and a story of the image.

It's amazing to observe how the eyes greet us, accept us and express dissatisfaction or fear.

We all have experienced the eye roll when expressing an idea, or disapproval of an action. Some say we talk with our eyes.

Direct eye contact is a sure sign of truth and confidence. Obtaining that comfort level is difficult for some and impossible for others. If we are telling the truth and believe in ourselves our eyes should speak for us.

I remembering practicing a bible reading for my nephews wedding. As I read the words I tried to look up so I got use to reassuring the congregation that I was confident in the reading, and that I believed in what I was reciting. After many practice runs I was ready to deliver the words of the bible verse.

Of course nerves got the best of me but in my mind I continued to remind myself to look up. I did, maybe not the best I could do but I finished. Oh, at the end I almost fell on my ass as I took the two steps down off the alter.

Like a girl walking in heels for the first time, I certainly did not have a graceful exit. Although I did recover my almost slip and fall well.

Chapter 10

Pride

I remember going to my first Pride Festival in St. Pete Florida. It was an extremely hot summer day as we drove to the event. As we got closer to our destination I was amazed at the size of the crowds walking towards the parade route. We finally found a parking spot on a back street in a residential neighborhood. As we parked the car it was imperative we gathered our bottles of water and belongings before locking the car and starting our walk.

The crowds made me a bit uneasy, but large crowds typically do. Some of my anxiety came from the unknown since I never participated in a Pride Parade before. I was taking it all in and watching the many people following the same path.

As we approached the parade route the streets were blocked off to allow various vendors an opportunity to set up their booths. There were so many vendors and food booths in this area. It was an eye opener to see so many companies who came to support our community, many greeting parade goers with trinkets which displayed a logo of their company name. Most were key chains and of course bottles of water.

I was impressed to see many young professionals who dedicated the time to volunteer.

PAUL R. BECKER

Usually the news media portrays our community only by the extravagant who choose to express themselves in other ways, this does not represent a majority of who we are. They need to report on what this event is intended, not negatively.

To be honest when I first thought about going to the parade I was sure to see one side, but I was clearly wrong.

As the parade started the casts of many demonstrated various cultures, beliefs and preferences. It was the definition of Diversity. Many men and woman celebrating the existence of our accomplishments and the ongoing struggle to be accepted. This parade was no different from Mardi Gras celebrations in New Orleans, or Carnival in South America. These are people with a cause, celebrating together without hate or judgement. Our world could use a similar parade.

The parade went on for hours, and as each group passed in front of me I was met with guilt. Not for being there, but for allowing our media to portray these events in a shameless way. I suddenly realized I had missed out on this event for so many years.

Once the parade ended we continued to walk around the streets, speak with various vendors and parade goers. We met so many fascinating people along the way. Many shared their stories of coming out and several straight married couples who come every year to support 'me', 'us' and most important our community.

Sure we have extremes and people who choose to express themselves in various ways, but that's okay. It's self-expression and their choice. No matter who or what community we relate to everyone has a place and should feel comfortable.

As we drove away from the event and headed home I was truly happy I participated and proud of everyone who saved this date and participated. In any community celebration we all should feel welcome. It's time to tear down so many walls that separate us and join together in recognition of our lives. Celebrate together without judgement.

I am not a flamboyant person and I pride myself on remaining the true professional I try to be every day. Once in a while I let loose, turn on Madonna's Vogue and dance like I am on Solid Gold. Well, maybe not. But within all of us there is a moment to let loose and express ourselves. Most times I turn up the volume in my car, open the sunroof and play my music loud. I silently sing along but imagine myself on stage singing in front of a crowd. It could be my ultimate desire to be famous. But wait, I am famous, at least to me I am.

Chapter 11

March to A Different Drummer

We all march to a different beat, some louder than others but our tune is unique. Some of us enter a room and heads turn because their tune is loud. Others come in softly like a low volume jazz tune. Of course there are few who stumble in, out of tune like an old 45 record that has scratches across it's vinyl. You know those types.

There is nothing wrong with any of these tunes, it's what makes us special. We have an opportunity in our lives to express ourselves in many ways. It could be the style of clothes we wear, our hair cut or simply the piece of jewelry we put on each morning. Regardless, we own it. Our way to let everyone who sees us understand our style.

Each day when I get dressed I put on a watch, typically on my left hand and a ring on the index finger of my right hand. The ring represents a commitment I made to the relationship I am in, and the devotion to the person I share my life.

Many have asked why my right hand vs my left. For me it was a matter of comfort and choice, does not change the symbolism. Normally we assume that a person wearing a ring on their left hand index finger is married. That's because it's tradition. Nothing wrong with tradition and there is room to change them too.

So my beat is different and my own. Although I like Top 40 music, I don't think it's appropriate to walk into a room to 'Star Boy' by The Weekend. Although it's one of my favorite songs.

We need to pick a beat and proceed with pride. Mostly comes down to soul searching and finding the inner self that has been repressed for a long time. Sometimes it takes a lifetime to find your inner spirit, but don't wait that long. Dig down deep and search for it, eventually you'll hear it. I did.

When I think about my beat and finding my inner self it took me longer than I would ever imagine. Took me 54 years! I have found my comfort in writing, which has helped me express my inner feelings, emotions and goals for life. I remember a quote by Beverly Cleary; "If you don't see the book you want on the shelf, write it."

My entrance song and beat is the sound of a marching band coming up the street in a Community Day Parade. The sound echoing off the buildings and the excitement of the crowd hearing the drum line keeping beat. That's me! The beat so heavy you feel it in your chest, it sends chills throughout your body.

It's how I see my future and what lies ahead.

I honestly look forward to growing older and becoming the wealth of knowledge my parents, grandparents, aunts and uncle are to me. My stories will be different and many will make you laugh and some may bring tears to your eyes. Knowing I have the ability to share one day with Chris and Emily or Jess and Blaire's children is an honor.

Chapter 12

Pay It Forward

There comes a time when we need to share our successes and pay forward to those who may need help. Paying forward comes in many forms, it does not necessarily mean you have to donate money.

These days it is more and more expensive just to survive. So what about giving up some of your time? Maybe an hour or two a month, twice a month. It's whatever you are comfortable giving and we all have time to give.

Sit back and think of the hours you spend watching 'Two Broke Girls' reruns, or the countless episodes of the 'Golden Girls.' I could watch episodes of both shows over and over. But ultimately the 'Golden Girls' takes precedence.

If you reflect on how many minutes spent paging through Facebook to get an update on all your friends to only get pissed about a post you don't care for, that energy could be used to help others. It's true and I encourage everyone to stop and think about it.

I finally realized this reality and decided to make a difference and share my time and do something rewarding. Not only to feel better about myself, but a sense of gratification of helping others. One hour a month is easy to give up for a cause we strongly believe in. That simple gesture goes a long way.

If everyone was given credit for community service, I would bet as a Nation we would accomplish so much. Many companies allow individuals time away from their jobs to give back in our communities, and we need more of it.

Think about it, search inside and figure out how you can help someone or your community. Count the useless minutes each day wasted sitting doing a meaningless task. Add that time and give it back. The personal reward is worth every minute.

Cannot say for sure when this simple reality came to my mind, or why it took so long to surface. My passion now is to make a difference and I hope family and friends follow my lead.

We need good leaders now in our world. If we work together these gestures of kindness will go a long way and unite us as our Founding Fathers intended many years before us.

As Denzel Washington said; "At the end of the day, it's not about what you have or even what you've accomplished. It's about who you've lifted up. Who you've made better. It's about what you've given back".

Chapter 13

Spiritual Side

Each of us has a spiritual side. We can choose to privately speak to those who have passed onto another life. What you decide is your choice.

Every day I speak in silence to my parents, friends and family members who have left this world. I look for direction, I ask for support and I thank all of them for making me the man I am today.

My conversations are brief but I look for signs to know they hear me. Sitting in silence for a moment is my peace, it's the time I take to simply say; "thank you".

There is an inner voice in each of us, it speaks in times of need and the jolt we feel occasionally is a reminder it is listening. I strongly believe our Creator has given us this inner being to guide our lives.

We have spirits among us too. They are our guardian angels who watch over us every day and keep us safe. You know they are there when that slight breeze hits the back of your neck when you walk into a dark room. The hair on the back of your neck tingles as your guardian angel passes by and their hand slightly touches your shoulder. Or the voice you thought you heard at the moment you are quietly sitting alone in your home. All of us has had those experiences. Sometimes that inner voice and angel tell us our decisions are not the best, and stop us to re-think our actions. In our mortal lives we title it as intuition.

No matter what you believe to be true, or how you choose to express those inner most feelings, you have a right to make the rules. No one can tell you if your right or wrong, it's what works for you. Those are your beliefs.

Spirituality comes in many forms and understanding the importance of finding your inner most beliefs is important. It could be that moment you close your eyes and escape to a place of calm and relaxation. The moment you are sitting at the beach, looking out over the Gulf of Mexico and imagining you are sailing off into the horizon. The few seconds you feel as if you are the only person on the beach with the sound of waves slapping into the sand.

At those moments we reflect on our lives and remember our past. It's a special moment to regenerate our souls and become comfortable with our inner voice. Listen closely as your Angel will make sure your journey is fulfilling.

Chapter 14

Life is a Puzzle

At some point we have worked on a jigsaw puzzle. In most circumstances we gathered around a table with family and friends to begin the task of connecting each piece to form the image that is displayed on the box cover. Many of us find it relaxing to build a puzzle alone.

Whether the puzzle has 500 or 1,000 pieces we usually begin by separating the flat edges from the remaining pieces. We begin by building the frame. It's important to take note of the edges too, those pieces usually get placed in the corners so a framework begins to form.

As we select pieces to fill in the middle we tend to hold them up to the picture on the box cover to identify where they could fit. It's a daunting task but slowly we begin to connect the pieces. The process sparks conversation and we begin to share thoughts and ideas of where we place each piece.

That's where I begin to think of how the puzzle compares to our lives. Early on the framework is built, we know our boundaries but our inner self is trying to fit in. Not always an easy task but we continue on. We cannot force someone to 'fit in' and we have to accept that when a connection is made, we accept the image they are connecting to. Just like a puzzle, you cannot force a piece. It has to connect naturally to the next one who supports it.

We cannot force anyone to alter their existence to be accepted, it has to fit according to the plan. The image we see when all the pieces are connected, is what we accept. The person who invented each piece of the puzzle intended to make sure all the pieces in a box come together. You cannot borrow from another puzzle.

As we begin to identify who we are, the outer frame of our lives begins to form. I see the frame as our family, friends and people who will support us. They hold us together.

We begin to form a connection with those supporting us as the image of who we are comes together. No one on that outer framework can force us to connect in a different direction, they have to accept us as we start forming our lives and complete the puzzle. Never at any time do we force someone to fit in if that piece is not a perfect fit. We accept every connection without judgement.

We don't judge a puzzle by its image. After all, you purchased it because you were drawn by an image of what it will become once all the pieces are firmly together.

Chapter 15

Design It & Live It

In our relationships we have an opportunity to design it how we feel it should be. Although most see us as unconventional, we tend to view it as trivialized. We have the ability to design what works best for us. Anyone has that option if you agree to live it and be respectful of each other. No one should ever feel afraid or embarrassed to express their opinions.

From the movie Too Wong Foo; **Miss Chi-Chi Rodriguez**: "Live life before it lives you."

We can break from tradition and design our lives and relationships as we see fit. In our relationships it takes more work and commitment. If we set the rules upfront it should not matter how we proceed.

There are many who express opinions of how we should live and love, but it's not their opinions which matters. Our relationship is stronger than most and because we work so hard to be accepted in our Communities I tend to think ours is more solid than most straight couples. Sure we don't have children and that is an option we tend to find more difficult. But we love our niece, nephews and their husband and wife's as our own.

Even in "straight" relationships some couples choose to not have children, and that is okay because it's what they designed as the framework of their relationship. Some judge those choices and feel these decisions are selfish. But it's not. So why do we judge? Maybe it's jealousy because two people spent time making sure how they want to proceed with the commitment they made with other works for them.

There are many couples who decide that "open relationships" are acceptable. I don't believe in it but support anyone who chooses that option. I support it only because two people together have made it a part of their relationship. Obviously they have spoken and set boundaries. It's not for me to judge. They designed it and live it.

Regardless of what you choose there is commitment. If you decide to have options great, just don't deviate from the design. Too many couples start off accepting the unknown and never communicate enough to express concerns or update the design. Any relationship requires a lot of talking and listening. We need to hear each other and be respectful when there are concerns.

In these day's couples have to work hard and stay focused. I have learned over the years that friends and family are important to our survival. Most important we all deserve alone time too. We need that time to reflect and as they say; "it makes the heart grow stronger."

When one of us is travelling we have committed to talk on the phone at least twice a day. I usually begin the day with a "wake up" call and to say "have a good day." Our second call is after our working day just to check in and see if we both had a nice day and talk about what happened that day. Our calls are not long, we designed this approach to know each other is safe.

I did a lot of travelling for work in the past. Usually my schedule was to leave on Monday and back on Friday. At one point in my career I worked out of state for 12 months. Hardest thing I ever did. It was lonely and the most depressing time of my life. However, it was a decision to progress my career but maintain our relationship and home in Pittsburgh. At no point during that time did I ever give up focusing on our commitment to each other. It had to work because I said it would. I had to live up to it.

After many flights home on the weekends I began to plan my departure from Atlanta to return to Pittsburgh and get back to what was most important. In the end through the struggles and certainly many sleepless nights our relationship stood strong.

You hear so many similar stories of couples who make this choice to live in separate states because of their careers. It is a life decision that could have negative consequences. Not easy and it takes two strong individuals to stay focused on the most important aspect of a relationship.

Although you "designed it and live it" there will be temptations that potentially could separate the bond between two adults. It's not easy out there and jealousy is ugly. Make sure you talk and be open and honest, never be afraid to speak your mind. Relationships take a lot of work and the best one's have lived through many challenges.

Sometimes our 'design' requires a good eraser to make edits. There is nothing wrong to make changes as you see fit as long as both parties agree to the direction you wish to take. Relationships are hard at times and if you listen to one another they become easy to manage.

It is certainly a "give and take." Remember it takes two to succeed.

Chapter 16

It's Just Me

Writing this book has given me a sense of satisfaction and has allowed me to express many years of hidden emotions. It has been a long road and I have come to the point to pull into a rest stop and reflect on a wonderful journey thus far.

In our childhoods we are introduced to so many people who have influences on upbringing. No one can determine our final destiny but they give us a map to follow. We can stay on track and follow the road signs or experiment with a detour that may bring us back to our original route.

Some choose to stay on track and never take in the scenery. That's okay.

My dad used AAA Trip Ticks when it was family vacation time. Did not matter if we went to the same Beach every summer, he had to get a road map. I remember my mom would sit in the passenger seat with my sister and me in the back seats. My mom would read the map and AAA would use a variety of stamps to indicate road construction or detours. Mom would let Dad know when the next exit was coming and what attractions were nearby. Sure, there were those times Dad was not listening and we continued down the highway past the exit. We would turn around at the next exit and come back around. Finally, back on track.

Eventually we would make it to our destination and the trip tick was carefully tucked away in the glove box of our Pontiac Catalina. At the time I never realized on the back side of the trip tick was the reverse directions that would get us home.

When Dad passed away we found a cabinet in his home filled with the trip ticks from many vacations. He saved every one.

Thinking of my own journey at 54 years old I tend to compare my life to those trip ticks. They begin with a starting point and finally lead us to our destination. The flip side of those maps lead us back home to one day be together at home (Heaven).

My trip tick had many detours and posed lots of challenges so far. Sure I made mistakes, took the wrong exit and even got a flat tire or two. I did not always have Mom reading the map to me but I continue to drive on and after some stops I get back on the right path.

It was more difficult to keep so many secrets from family and friends but at those moments I was driven to be accepted. In the past I felt my acceptance would have been met with disappointment and no one would open their arms to welcome me. At that time in my life it truly was a choice I made.

If I could teach anyone having difficulty with feeling accepted I say be honest. Often times people have difficulty with honesty and thrive on making assumptions that potentially cause more harm to everyone's well-being.

The journey I am on has lead me to a destination that has allowed me to be proud and more comfortable with who I am today. Coming into the second half of my life I can see that my trip tick is a map of acceptance and I begin a journey home. My trip has been fulfilling so far and I can honestly say I have seen and done a lot to get myself to this point. Now on the reverse side I have many more things to see. Just as we follow a map to our vacation destination we tend to stay focused on a timeframe to arrive, we don't spend enough time enjoying the sites. It's only because our time is limited. When we take time away from work we are limited to how many days we have to enjoy vacation.

But in life our road map home should be filled with sightseeing and moments to last a lifetime.

Chapter 17

It All Comes Together

Every Sunday morning, I plug in an iron and select the clothes I will wear to work for the week. I match each shirt with a pair of pants and begin the process to iron out every wrinkle. Kyle laugh's because I even iron my shirts after they come back from a dry cleaner. But for me it's my trademark. It's what I do and it makes me feel good about myself.

I have even been known to re-iron my clothes if they get wrinkled throughout the day and I am going to continue wearing an outfit for dinner that night. Okay, maybe a little over the edge. A 'little'.

Each morning during the week I have my routine; wake up around 4:45am to 5:00am, go to the kitchen, pour my cup of coffee and turn on the news. For about 30 minutes I sit alone watching the news. When I hear footsteps upstairs I pour Kyle his coffee and get Madison's breakfast ready (our dog).

Around 5:30am I go back upstairs to shave, shower and get dressed. In my mind I know which outfit I ironed on Sunday will be worn on Monday, Tuesday, Wednesday, Thursday or Friday. In my plan to iron I try to line up the outfits by day of the week. Still with me? You do that too right?

Once dressed I come down the stairs and get my breakfast, usually yogurt, banana and orange juice. After my morning ritual it is time to gather my things and leave for work. My morning is no different than anyone else, we all have different morning rituals and I think most are similar to mine/ours.

We typically talk about the local news stories and briefly discuss any errands we need to run once we get home. I sometimes mention my idea for dinner and that I have thawed out a meat choice to cook. On some occasions we have a moment to walk Madison together as the sun is about to come up over Kensington Court. It's another opportunity to talk and reflect on what our expectations for the day will be. It's no different than our neighbors, family or friends.

In many housing developments couples start their days in a similar fashion. Our timing might be a bit different as we have the ability to re-arrange our schedule as long as getting to the end result is met.

Chapter 18

Self-Worth

I use to think that self-worth was measured by how much money you had or the total value of the material things you possessed. You know the old saying; "keeping up with the Jones'". Boy, was I wrong. There is so much more to that definition.

I strongly believe it stands for a state of mind and the value you place on knowing who you are; it's about confidence in yourself and what motivates you. What drives you every day and the satisfaction you get. Self-worth comes when you have identified who you truly are and the accomplishments you achieve.

Self-worth comes with knowing you have made a mark in society and have gained the respect of your peers. It comes with knowing you hold your head high and believe in 'YOU.' It comes with RESPECT! That is Self-Worth.

If you can honestly say yes to each example you should be proud. Self-worth is an accomplishment we should all strive for, it makes you feel good about yourself. It builds confidence and others notice.

We travel on a spiritual journey during our lives, we are met with temptations and are asked to make life decisions that are more difficult than others. If you understand why we are met with these choices it seems to make sense, it defines who we become. In later years we share the journey to leach lessons of success and moments of failure. No one can say they have had a lifetime of success, if they did then I feel certain they are lacking in self-worth. For every one positive moment there has to be a negative, we learn from those examples.

Our self-worth increases over time, we add to it in the simplest of ways and most often don't recognize our value grew. Not like we can look on-line for our deposit total.

Throughout our lives we tend to build friendships with new people, we also lose friendships as others tend to move on and interests change. The people who we are closest to tend to hold on a lifetime because they add value in our lives. They teach us and help us to grow. Same holds true in our families.

Sometimes we let people go as the original value they once had begins to decrease. They no longer hold a place in our lives that offer support which enables us to grow. Over time and throughout life it happens.

Similar to making a bank deposit. The transaction is knowledge and our accounts represent our self-worth. Each deposit increases the value of our account, as we take money out and see our balance decrease we look for more knowledge from others who offer value to replace what is left. The withdrawal represents someone who drains our self-worth because we spend more money or time forcing it to work that we lose value.

Over time our goal is to grow the account and earn interest. When I think of interest we earn I equate that to experience. The more we add experience and knowledge together we see a benefit and a lifetime of an interest bearing account can be powerful.

As they say; "Knowledge is Power".

Try growing your account, make it powerful and keep earning interest. For every withdraw you make replace it with a deposit that will exceed your expectations.

Chapter 19

My Reflections

We are living in a world that continues to leave many of us scratching our heads in disbelief. Our Leaders are not upholding the values that our Founding Fathers created in order for us to live and work together as a Nation united.

When you watch the News each night I am embarrassed at the behavior of those who take responsibility for our well-being. It scares me to think decisions are made on our behalf as I have no faith in those who lead us.

Certainly everyone needs to step back, listen to one another and come together so we can finally all live together for a common cause. Our Country is not working in its current state, and it's our role to help get it back on track. When we decide on leaders to represent us, it is not about a popularity contents, rather about values that we believe in and respect for everyone no matter their race, color, religion or sexual orientation.

It has to be about trust!

I'm not into political debates or posting my opinions on social media, but I do feel strongly that change is needed. We need to respect each other as individuals and not separate us by titles. Our representatives in Congress cannot hold discussions intelligently without taking sides of which party they support. Do they realize they live in the same world of the people who they tend to hurt the most? US!

Everyone living on this earth has a voice that needs to be heard. At no point should any living human being feel afraid to express themselves. Shame on those Leaders who prevent us from being open with our opinions.

Our Creator did not intend us to be silenced by men or woman who have no self-respect, who seek harm to others that don't follow their authority. If we follow the teachings that proceeded us, they are wrong.

We have a human right to be heard.

So many people recently have come out to express their positions on abuse, political opinions and in general the state of our Union. Regardless if we believe in their actions or personal experiences it's our responsibility to allow them to be heard. If we don't express the differences and beliefs we have our Nation and World will never improve, and lately and cannot get any worse.

People who have been silenced for decades need heard. It is our perceptions and threats of silence that allow individuals in leadership roles to control us.

Take action! Speak up!

Let's change our Nations and World and make it exist without barriers and hate. I realize we may never see 100% in our lifetime but working together will make this World a better place for our young generation.

So much will changed decades from now and the thought of bringing up children in this current environment is frightening.

Chapter 20

Your Name

Did you ever wonder how your name came to be? Sure, we know our parents assigned it to us at birth. But what was the thought behind it? I have heard friends and co-workers say they wish their name was......, or they have met someone with a cool name that they wish was their own. Of course some names keep us wondering as to why would anyone name their child that. I'm sure you can relate to one of those conversations.

Thinking back and imagining how our parents felt when they learned a new life was about to come into their lives, the excitement and planning happened for months before we actually came into this World. Our parents planned to give us a title that would be most suitable to represent the family, and carry on the legacy of the family name. Most times our middle name were easy to define, as in most cases it represents a parent or grandparent. Mine is my Father's first name.

Finally, our parents agree to our first name and we carry that title for a lifetime. It's our identity to the World and we should be honored since the choice has meaning. No one should ever want to change their name, as it defines who we are. Although the meaning of my name does not necessarily fit; at 6'3" I don't think the definition of Paul, which means "small" agrees. But I am proud to hold the title.

Many get creative with names and go 'out of the box' when awarding their child a family title. Over time we have accepted those names and even though we sometimes struggle to pronounce them, somehow they hold meaning to the parents. It defines them as unique and special.

Growing up I used to imagine being named after my grandfather; his name was Leo. Figured that would have been a cool name for me. We sometimes think our names should change because in various 'slangs' our name is pronounced different and certainly not necessarily flattering. So if our name was different would anything have changed for us? It's not our first name which defines how we learn and the person we become, surely is a title we have and work towards making others to take notice of who we are.

Being in a customer service role I often joke to say; "I am changing my name", only because of the many phone calls I receive from clients when issues are escalated. My staff will receive a call asking for "Paul".

Just like our Mothers use to say when we would call out; 'Mom, Mom'. Often my mother would say she was changing her name too. Little did she know we would eventually figure out her new name. If we did something wrong somehow our middle name was added when Mom or Dad demanded our attention. Now that is when I wish I could change my name. I can still hear the echoing of 'Paul Robert' throughout the house. Usually I forgot to do something I promised would be done.

One of the funny moments we can relate to is when Mom would get mad for some reason or another, but in the heat of the moment we became the dog's name, our sisters name or the kid down the street. Eventually Mom would say; "you know who you are" and then burst into laughter. At that point the emotion of anger turned to a moment of laughter as Mom knew she just blew it then. No recovery could change the fact she forgot who I was. I miss those days.

Even though I am defined as 'small' I would never change my name, it defines who I am and will carry with me for a lifetime. As we have heard over and over; 'make a name for yourself,' in other words make sure people know who you are and define yourself by the person you become.

There are some who acquire a nickname too. It is a title which is unique to that individual. Most times it is given to us in our young adult years and for whatever reason it sticks with us until adulthood. The nickname is a characteristic that took thought and for whatever reason was chosen for us by friends or family.

My father's nickname was B-I-N-G-O. Our family gave him that title and for many reasons it fit. His close ties and devotion to the Catholic Church was a contributing factor, as we know those Catholics love their B-I-N-G-O. Kyle and I named our boat after my father. As we would float on the Allegheny River passing boaters used to yell out B-10, our response back was B-I-N-G-O. It was an honorable tribute to Dad.

In grade school I had the title of "Tall Paul", it was given to me by our school principal. Definitely an oxymoron given the true meaning of my name.

Be proud of your title and make the most of who you are. Leave your legacy for those who know and have met you along your journey. Let others speak of you and celebrate your life for decades after you leave this Earth. You are (NAME)!

Chapter 21

Measures of Time

Remember those sayings of; "time heals"; "it takes time"; "time flies when you are having fun." All some form of tracking time related to moments in our lives which potentially last a lifetime.

How often do we sit and wait for a response or at the doctor's office? It seems like that happens more often these days. The excitement of flying anywhere is met with the expectation of waiting. We begin to plan for those moments and add that time into our schedule. The measurement of time over our lives and the unused minutes could add up to a monumental amount.

What can we do to fill that unused time, and the minutes we wait let tick by us? Most often people read, talk on the phone or reflect on the day. If time flies by obviously we have accounted for every minute of our day. When minutes turn into hours and then days that time starts adding weight to our shoulders. We begin to lose hope and start thinking the waiting will never be over. At some point our personalities begin to change as a defense.

It takes a toll on anyone and at some point we give up. Similar to someone who wants acceptance or to feel appreciated for who they are. They express themselves and do what they feel is necessary to get noticed. Maybe several attempts to make a point and a statement of who they are inside. On the outside the clock ticks as they wait for a sign, a hug, a nod, the simple tap on their shoulder to say someone cares.

We watch the time go by every day and most days we wish that time would move more quickly. Those days are typically attributed to a bad day at work. Did you ever imagine what happens in a minute? You hear stories about; every minute there is a new birth. We all have heard them. I'm as guilty as anyone wishing time away.

In my life now I want it to slow down. I want to enjoy the time I have left on this earth. Time to treasure each moment and accept the good and bad days. I certainly look forward to tomorrow, but not because I wish today away.

I honestly wish I did not take so long to identify who I am. I can never get that time back. Cannot turn the clocks back and relive those moments.

I've come to a point where I do more silent reflection on my daily accomplishments. I sometimes play those moments over in my mind, not to change anything but to honestly think about how my decisions made a difference. Not always an easy task because I do reflect on moments that negatively impacted my day. Surely contributed to my bad day but added value to who I am and how other see me.

My reflections include what goals I have set for myself and a timeline of when I expect to achieve them. As I worked towards the day I can retire my aspirations of where I want to be in my career give me the drive for tomorrow.

Most days I wish for more time. So the sayings I mentioned do hold true. If we cut ourselves, it takes "time to heal." We watch the process as slowly the wound goes away. Sometimes we are left with a scar and a simple reminder of that injury.

Diversity and Acceptance are no different. It simply takes time.

Chapter 22

Imagination

I remember a friend I had back in my childhood years who stayed with me until I was in grade school. His name was Michael Jimmy. When I think back I recall talking to him at moments I needed to reach out and feel secure. Although Michael Jimmy seemed to come and go, I knew he was there for me. He did not argue or insist on getting his way, he was patient and never judged me. In some ways I felt at any time I needed him, he would be there.

You see, Michael Jimmy was the imaginary friend I created. I told my Mom about him and often times when I was alone in my room we spoke, it was make believe and in my mind he was my true friend. When I was sad I could reach out and ask that he just listen. He was a calming voice who accepted me for who I am.

Whether or not you once created an imaginary friend, I'm sure all of us at one time or another spoke to anyone who would listen in silence. Our minds are remarkable and what it can teach us can be overwhelming at best. The mind and spirit work hand in hand and how we process what we are being taught can be rewarding. Creativity at its simplest form is becoming a lost art. In my sub-conscious I created Michael Jimmy to fill a void when I could not interact with the mortal friends I had. It's amazing to understand how we program ourselves to believe in someone who only exists in our imagination.

Paracosm is the term used to describe the phenomenon of an imaginary friend. It is also a sign of being very creative, so for me it helped to find my true self and express feelings that I was not able to share with mortals. This was the beginning of who I have become. I surely do not keep in touch with Michael Jimmy any longer, maybe he moved and I know he does not have a Facebook page. It all comes back to what makes us unique. At one point in my earlier years I needed someone I could trust and share my inner most secrets with and at that time it worked.

No matter if we choose to create an image of a person we can in our mind relate to, or we have a close human person who just simply listens, it comes down to a choice. There is no right or wrong answer and no one can take that away from you. We dream good thoughts and paint images of a perfect existence. Sure it is fun at the time and somehow it all works. We know as we get older that a perfect existence is met with uncertainty. Sometime we fight to be accepted and maybe calling up those imaginary friends from the past for support isn't so bad. Well, okay, maybe be careful because others may think you went off the deep end.

Whatever you decide, be truthful with yourself and never be afraid to share your story. It's important to let others know what worked for you and hopefully it pays forward. For every person we help, the choices they make will seem much easier.

It's about existence together with no barriers.

That silent moment when we look up at the sky and speak quietly to those we have known and who are looking over us is a special time no none can take from us. I often reflect on how each of those individuals has mentored me and what they have done to inspire my life. Often times I wish to have an hour back with each person to describe who I have become. Just so they know. I know, crazy right? One of my co-workers speaks to her friends who have passed on, she wishes them Happy Birthday and asks for support in times of need. Funny she shares that with me but its real.

Chapter 23

Humble

The act of being humble is something that is taught to us over our lifetime. Some will never experience it and others will live it forever. It surely is an honor and many more need to grasp the rewards. Not easy to set aside the perceptions of how others see us and bring ourselves down a few levels once in a while. Honestly the experience opens your eyes and gives you an appreciation for many who have not taken time to recognize.

At the height of my career I took a hard knock down and to financially see my way through I began working at a local grocery store. The first day of orientation was hard, I could not comprehend what I was about to do as I reflect back on my journey so far. As the job requirements were described I began to feel a sense of anxiety, I wanted to run. Looking around the room I began trying to imagine how these other new employees got here too.

My new job was working in the 'hot foods' department serving food, cleaning tables and emptying trash. I wore a uniform now and it felt strange. My career I once had seemed like a dream that I may not ever live out again. It took me time to meet everyone in the department and finally I began to open up. I was a bit nervous but I was finding comfort in my co-workers. In this new reality I was not alone.

Now working with the public I began to observe and witness so much. Some of the customers were incredibly rude to me and my co-workers. The store was in a higher class neighborhood, most wives did not work and many thought you owed them the World. You know, the 'ME' syndrome. The men who shopped at the store and came into the department were obviously sent with a shopping list but had no idea on what they really needed to buy. I would simply bite my tongue and do my best to compose myself. I had to for I was an employee and was trained to respect the customer.

After a few months I met a gentleman who came into the store every morning for coffee. He liked a certain flavor and I began to memorize the exact proportions of sugar and milk. Like clock-work I knew when he was coming and would prepare his drink. After a few times he remarked how appreciative he was and amazed I did that for him. One day he said; "you don't belong here." I looked at him and asked; "why don't you think so?" Simply put his reply was "I can tell by your demeanor and professional appearance." I began to explain my journey and how I now became a clerk in 'hot foods'. He listened to every word, never interrupted and never judged me. This man was interested in 'me'. At the end of our discussion he thanked me for sharing and shook my hand. He then said; "taking this job has to be a humbling experience for you." It finally hit me and I realized my purpose.

Every day after our conversation I had a fresh coffee waiting and we spoke about my efforts to get back into Banking. He encouraged me and supported my efforts. Every day he shook my hand and said; "thank you." At this point in my life what I was doing had to do with survival. It was my soul searching and an opportunity to listen and observe. I was gaining a new appreciation for anyone in this industry dealing with the public. It was amazing how disrespectful people can be to one another. If only people would think for a moment before they humiliate someone who is doing their best to survive and make a living waiting on them. It was an incredible experience and forced me to see people as individuals, not by the uniform they wear or the counter they stand behind. They are people who demand as much respect as 'me'.

Chapter 24

I Did Nothing Wrong

I use to believe that being gay meant you were punished because of something you did wrong and this was how our creator was testing me. Early on I thought the feelings would go away and if I said enough prayers I could be cured. The first time I stepped into a gay bar I figured something bad would happen to me. Funny thing was I had an experience that tested my theory, although just a coincidence.

One night my friend Chas and I went to a bar in the Oakland area of Pittsburgh. We took my father's car as mine was in the shop. This was after my divorce and finally I was ready to see what this lifestyle was all about. I was nervous and had no idea what to expect. I picked Chas up and off we went. I pulled into the parking lot and found an open space behind the Bank which was closed. The bar patrons used this parking lot after hours. As we walked in the front door my heart was racing and I immediately headed towards the bar. The bartender was a young man who was very friendly and I got the sense he knew I was new to this scene. After I got my drink we walked around the bar and found an opening at the pool tables. Soon after we were joined by others who wanted to play too. Actually, it was starting out to be a fun night. I met some great people and we laughed and talked about so many things.

As the evening progressed I motioned to Chas it was time to go. We said our goodbye's and headed back to the front door. When we walked towards the car I noticed a problem, the car was gone. There was broken glass where the car was parked and I started to panic, this was my father's car. We figured a call to the police was in order because I had to report the car stolen. I was on the phone with the police and Chas was calling us a cab so we could get back home. The plan was I was spending the night at his house.

After I filed the police report the cab came and we started home. This was before cell phones so I had to call my father, but would wait until the morning as it was after 2:00 am. Once we arrived at Chas' parent's home we sat on their back porch, lit up a cigarette and began laughing uncontrollably. I think it was a reaction to this night and the sense of reality of how this all happened. Eventually we went into the house and both fell asleep.

I woke up only after a few hours of sleep to only lay in bed and stare at the ceiling. I wondered if this was my sign. Why did I go there and is this for me? Was this my payback? My head was spinning. I was trying to digest the previous night and now had to call my father.

Once Chas woke up, we had breakfast with his stepmother and only told that the car was stolen and never said we went to a gay bar. I told Chas to drive me home and I would handle the conversation on my end.

The conversation about the car went better than I thought. Of course I never said where I went, only mentioned that we were in Oakland. My father was actually pretty calm as he said there is nothing I could have done to prevent it and hopefully the car would be found. That was a weight off my shoulders. It was three weeks and his car was found. There was minor damage but nothing that could not be fixed. Whomever stole the car left a six pack in the back seat. The car was repaired and soon life went back to normal.

From that point on I began to blame myself and thought my actions of that night contributed to the situation of the car. I repeated that night over and over and tried to understand what I did wrong. Was it the bar?

Maybe someone I spoke with knew me and this was their revenge? All sorts of scenarios played over and over again.

Finally; it hit me. I did nothing wrong. I could not have prevented the car from being stolen. This was my first night of the lifestyle I was finally comfortable with. Although to this day I don't really enjoy bars, it was the patrons at that bar I had things in common with and will for the rest of my life. For some reason I felt safe there because I was no longer hiding behind a false identity.

It should not matter where we choose to socialize or the bar that allows us to be open in our sexuality. Life is way too short and feeling we did something wrong that lead us to this lifestyle is exhausting. Everyone one has to be accepted in this World.

Chapter 25

Message in A Bottle

Did you ever send a message in a bottle? Or maybe you found one? Normally we don't look for empty bottles along the shore line that could potentially contain a message, and maybe no one ever does. Somewhere it has happened and the person who performed this stunt took time to write an important message to anyone who would listen. Could be inner most thoughts, or asking for help. Maybe the receiver of the bottle could win one million dollars. Fun to imagine but highly unlikely.

Whomever took the time to plan the launch of their message and bottle had to think about and plan every step. Obviously this individual needed to express themselves and wanted someone to accept them, or take ownership for the directions written on the paper. The originator would not have known a potential recipient or even if the current would send their bottle out into the water to travel miles until finding a resting place.

As this individual began to write they wrote from their heart, they anticipated the bottle being found and fantasized about being contacted. The ultimate end result of the bottles journey. Once the note was placed inside, the cork would be securely tapped into place. Of course the right launching point would be chosen, one with no obstructions. Usually before being launched the creator of this memorable event would have a few words of reflection. Normally a quick silent prayer and then toss the bottle into the water. This individual would watch until the bottle was out of sight, then slowly they would turn from the shore and head back home.

As hours and days would pass the anticipation of waiting would consume the sender. Months would pass and finally the bottle and message were a past act of courage and commitment. The sender would have periods of emotional thoughts as they truly believed in their destiny.

Same holds true to feelings of acceptance. We struggle to find the right words as we seek approval and pray for someone to simply notice us. The words we use to identify with hold value to what we strongly believe in. Waiting for someone to hear our words and acknowledge our existence can weigh heavily on our shoulders.

If our bottle never reaches the shore and is picked up and read, we go on deflated that no one will ever understand who we are. I'm not saying we all need to launch a message in a bottle, I am saying don't allow someone to wait for your acceptance and commitment. Hear their message. Everyone has a personal message to be heard. Whether the path takes days, months or years it's important to acknowledge.

When we toss the bottle into the water it's like announcing and letting go of a secret which has been bottled up inside. The initial toss of the bottle determines how we proceed. If the bottle floats and is picked up by the current, we are lifted and carried through until our final resting point. When the bottle struggles to stay afloat we tend to work harder as our goal is the regain our approach and slowly hold our heads above the water until we some to a point we no longer struggle to survive. Symbolism is a powerful tool and digging deep to understand the meaning behind it can open our eyes. So much of what we do and how we live our lives is taught to us by simple gestures of reflection.

Carry your message forward and look to share the thoughts that will lead you to feeling good about yourself. Never worry about your journey, if your head is held high you will recognize the best place to rest and be comfortable. At the end of the journey someone will hold you tight and cherish you.

Chapter 26

Out of The Closet

As a kid I loved to watch scary movies. One of my favorites was Halloween with Jamie Lee Curtis. I remember the excitement of watching the movie and waiting for the moments when Michael Myers would appear. It was fun to yell at the TV as if the characters on the screen knew you were telling them to hide. In almost every scene someone would run into the closet, it was their safe zone. At least for a moment. How did Michael Myers know to always look there? It was the movies and it contributed to the scene and made your adrenaline rush. However, you knew coming out of the closet was a risk, even looking through the key hole to validate a clear path was a risk. Jamie Lee would slowly open the door, we would hold onto the seat cushions in anticipation, waiting for Michael Myers to strike again. After Jamie Lee would escape and could see the daylight there was a moment of relief, she survived another night. We sat back in the sofa and regrouped until the next encounter.

When I began to understand my true self and hearing terms associated with being gay I cringed with the term; "out of the closet." You wonder why? Not because I had nightmares of Michael Myers, but it was the fear of the unknown. What will it be like when I emerge from that open door? Sitting in the dark for so long leaves you anticipating the worst. With each glance from the key hole you look for validation that the path is free from any obstacles which could stop you. So for me the term was met with a lot of anxiety and fear for the unknown.

It's one of the hardest things we do in our lives. The emotions we encounter can be overwhelming and consume us. Why is it we have those fears? Some choose to remain in the dark to occasionally glance out the key hole to asses a clear path. Those of us who have opened the door find relief in the fact we can be free of the dark and prepare ourselves for anyone who tries to push us back.

Truly it is the fear of not knowing, for many years we search for the right words and the best time to announce our 'coming out'. The waiting is painful because we hide from reality and pretend we fit in. The moment we escape from the darkness should be a celebration of freedom. It's why we gather each year for 'PRIDE'.

Many are left behind in the dark constantly looking through the key hole, they sit in darkness because they know their ability to open that door will be met with failure. That is what we need to change. We can identify a family member, friend or co-worker struggling to 'come out', take time to reassure them it's okay and they have our support. Don't let someone we care for suffer, make the first move and unlock the door. Show them the path to freedom. That weight of not knowing what will be is huge.

I struggled for many years to finally escape the darkness. I looked through the key hole to see when I could safely 'come out'. It took many years but finally I saw a clear path and knew it was time. It was a rewarding experience to close that door and lock it forever, as I would never allow myself to feel ashamed of who I am. Sure my path was not free of obstacles but perseverance helped to guide me.

Today I am secure in who I am, confident as to what I plan for the future and certainly I have hands of support guiding me along the way.

Just like the movie, there was always a happy ending and we look forward to the sequel. My only advice; "lock those doors!"

Chapter 27

In the Scheme of Things

At the end of the day what really matters? It's the way things happen and all things considered, truly is the definition of the statement. I think it is one of those statements that we struggle to find an appropriate response to. Really it has a deep meaning if you take time to understand the implication. It can be used to describe many situations, relationships or our society. We tend to dwell on making simple acts into major issues, most times we tend to worry or react without fact or knowledge and assume the worst. Surely our human nature.

Why is that? Can we take control and identify with truths and not label based on assumption? Because 'in the scheme of things' does it matter? Interesting! I equate this to my relationship and others similar to mine.

Early on we worry about making others happy with our choices and lose focus on what really matters. We tend to avoid the obvious and allow outside influences to determine who we should become. It does not matter if you are Gay or Straight it happens to everyone at one point or another. Sometimes we protect our 'partners' from the being brought into situations which become uncomfortable or present themselves with ongoing questions of why or why not. Surely those close to us want to express their opinions to only protect us from what could be a hardship, they have our best interest at heart.

Opinions do matter and expressing them can be rewarding, but we have to listen closely. Don't be afraid to express yours too. No one wants to be hurt or misunderstood, and what really matters in any relationship is that others respect us. Sometimes people close to our inner circle see things we don't. But keep your eyes open and stay observant.

Relationships are tough enough without having to appease others. Sometimes the effort is daunting and the efforts seem to be exhausting. But if it is meant to be it will happen. All things considered we have to be happy and our partners have to be accepted for better and worse.

Chapter 28

Channel Surfing

Usually on the weekend I begin the daunting task to find something light hearted to watch on TV. You would think with a 200 channel cable package that would be a simple task. I start on channel number 241 and work my way backwards. Amazing the content of what is available these days on cable TV, actually think I could write a self-help book on that topic. As I continue my search for just the right program I usually find myself watching re-runs of old sitcoms. The oldies but goodies. My ultimate go to Saturday morning show is the Golden Girls. I never get tired of Sophia, Rose, Dorothy and why would you not love Blanche.

The series began in 1985 and certainly was a hit from the beginning. At that time, I was 22 years old. I can remember sitting in my Grandparents living room watching the show. We would laugh and imagine ourselves living in St. Olaf. Although I don't think that Town would be ready for me. I can remember the episode when the girls travelled to Rose's hometown, it took days and the final journey was a horse and carriage ride down a dirt path. Rose called out into the darkness to let her friend know they were arriving.

Those 4 women had a unique bond and were drawn to each other for a reason. They shared stories, gave each other a hard time for various reasons but never turned their backs in a time of need. Sure, they expressed their opinions but never judged each other for the lives they chose to live. These 4 women were teaching us a lesson.

No matter who came into their lives they each shared opinions and as a drawn together family of friends they always had discussions over cheesecake at the kitchen table. Maybe the cheesecake was their form of a magic eight ball. Sure they had road bumps and struggles along the way but these friends stuck together.

I used to imagine having great friends to share our senior years with just like the show. And why not? I can picture which of my closest friends resemble each character. Funny to imagine. I can honestly say that I have each photo of the Golden Girls handing in our home. I guess I am obsessed with these women.

No matter how you view the show and which episode was your favorite, each held a deep meaning and lesson. My favorite episode is when Sophia travelled back to the home she raised her children. She searched for the lines marked in the wood trim that measured the timeline of Dorothy and her brother's growth. She also reflected and spiritually spoke to her husband Sal. The journey was tough for Sophia because she was searching for signs from her past as she grows older and her memory begins to test her.

As I watch that episode today I find the hidden meaning of family, sharing our past with the young generation that proceeds us. The most important is never stop talking to those who no longer walk on this earth. Keep memories alive.

After Sophia finally found what she wanted to see she felt a sense of relief and fulfillment. As she shared the memories with Dorothy it brought them closer together. Once again after a long journey to New York the girls sat around the kitchen table and ate dessert as Dorothy shared their adventure.

PAUL R. BECKER

It is amazing to hear how others grew up and hear how their families
came to be. I was fortunate to spend time with both sets of Grandparents
and would never regret those memories. My mother's parents lived four
doors down from our home, my father's parents lived on the other side
of the city. Both sets of Grandparents were amazing. I miss them dearly.

Chapter 29

Carnival Time

O nce a year our community and parish came together for the Church Carnival. It took months of planning and long nights of preparation. The carnival committee came together and did their due diligence on what worked the previous year and what should change for this year's event. There were trips to the local distributor to select prizes and pick which games would be played. That was my favorite part of this entire planning process. I got to decide on which stuffed animals I liked the most, there were rooms filled with every variety of lions, tigers and bears. Oh my!

In the parking lot of the Church the parishioners began assembling the game stands, food booths and prepared the lot for the arriving carnival rides. It was an exciting time of the year and usually the Carnival was in the Summer months. We would spend hours each night preparing for opening night.

My Mom usually worked in the Cottage located on the Church property, she was part of the team who counted the money each night. My Dad was the Deacon and would be in charge of coordinating schedules to make sure each booth had enough workers. He would walk the lot every night and keep the Carnival going.

I can remember my favorite game. In the middle of the stand there was a multi-level platform with a variety of glassware lined up in rows. Some glasses were taller than others and all sorts of colors and shapes. The goal was to toss a time into a glass and the prize was the glassware the dime landed inside. As you played the game the goal ended up being how many of the same types of glasses you could win and make a complete set. Of course you could trade pieces along the way. I actually worked the booth once or twice.

Once the crowds left we would walk the lot and go in and out of each booth. Most nights we waited until the final numbers were calculated and the currency was secure.

Each night the parking filled with the hum of laughter and sounds of people having a good time. There were no fears, no threats and everyone was comfortable being in a crowd of people who only wanted to support the Parish. It was a gathering place.

So why in today's World we use metal detectors or police patrolling events to ensure we are safe? It's hard to imagine what has brought us to this point. People change, our environment changes and we accept a new world.

We have become so wrapped up in our own space that we don't engage together, not only as families, but individuals. These events of the past are no longer appreciated or thought to be opportunities to unite as a community. In tragic events we seem to come together only to express our feelings for poor judgement and actions taken by others that leave families heartbroken.

Since those days of the parish carnivals I have not gone to a community fair in a long time. Maybe because of the memories that I cherished or simply because I would be disappointed as to what they have become today. For me in my 50's now I don't like large crowds and I feel at risk being in them. So I choose to observe from a distance. Why have we come to this point?

Most of what we are afraid of is a constant reminder on the daily news. The media portrays these events over and over to the point that analyst draw conclusions that make us think twice. Our World is no longer without eyes in every corner. Our privacy has been taken away and the next person in line who commits a horrible act wants to top his/ her predecessor.

We show too much.

Chapter 30

The Big Game

As everyone lined up on the basketball court we were split into two single forming lines facing each other. The gym teacher proceeded to designate who the captains of each team would be, usually the most popular guys got that title. Each captain stood at the head of each line and the process of picking their team began. No set rules on how long this exhausting task would take but as a player it felt like a lifetime. When the names were called the players would high five the captain and stand behind him encouraging who would make the cut. The best players were chosen first and it was clear who were the "in guys". In some ways this was a deflating experience because it truly set each player apart by popularity and not necessarily their ability to play the sport.

Normally I would make the 4th or 5th cut, mainly because of my height. I played the sport and was on the team but I was not in a starter position when we played against other schools. I was fine with that because I knew playing sports was not my first choice. Once everyone was chosen the team captains gathered us together and we talked about which positions we would play. Now a coin was tossed and the teams were distinguished by shirts and skins. Oh how I hated that. It was obvious that shirts meant you kept a shirt on and skins meant you took yours off.

The game would go on for 30 minutes until the bell would ring to signal the end of gym class. We had 15 minutes to shower and change back into our school clothes and the teams that took half the period to choose became separated and no one really seemed to care. Some of the guys thrived on their success in the game and of course would throw jabs at the losing team and those who missed a basket. It was what guys do in school.

I often wondered if the selection process was taught to Gym Teachers in College or was it a task they learned in the field. Did they ever really think about that task and how daunting it was? Were there ever thoughts on the impact to those who routinely were never chosen until the end or even the very last person being chosen out of the line. How depressing that would be.

Maybe this process does not happen now, and certainly I would be teams are not designated by 'shirts' and 'skins'. Unfortunately, in our World today someone would perceive it as sexual harassment. Oh how things have changed.

Reflecting back to this task I honestly can sympathize with those who were left alone in that line waiting to be chosen. The rejection of not hearing their name called to join the team had to weigh heavy on their ego. In their mind I can imagine that they tried to think of how to get noticed. Looking down the line from the standpoint of one who was chosen it was easy to recognize the heartache.

These are learned behaviors that follow us into adulthood. We don't necessarily recognize them until you really think back and apply it today. If you look at those who were not chosen it was a certain stereotypes; the "geek" or "brain of the class."

Chapter 31

Invited to The Dance

Growing up we faced many obstacles that would test our patients and secure our space on the most popular list. Usually we worked towards the highest honor which came with respect and a strong sense of confidence. Along with that title was a responsibility to be 'cool' and you began to develop a following, others wanted to be your friend. It takes a lot of work and it can be seen as arrogant or selfish. But its life and as young adults those are the games we play. Looking at it from another angle we don't always see who gets hurt.

I used the hate when the High School dances came along and the pressure was on to ask someone out for a date. Of course guys push each other about asking the popular girl, the cheerleader or the HOT girl who turned heads walking down the hall. Although the pressure was on the guy, each of those girls no matter their stature was equally under the same or more pressure. They had to make sure every day they looked especially nice just to entice the right guy who would ask them to the dance.

What about the quiet girl in the corner of the classroom who kept to herself? Or the guy who was the class geek that because of his approach would never have the nerve to ask a quiet girl out? Let's not forget the boys and girls who have not self-identified with themselves for fear of being rejected. The pressure for anyone in this situation is hard, emotions run wild and we begin to re-think our position on the popularity scale. But should that really matter?

Why do we have to work so hard for people to like us? *Answer:* We don't.

Early on we begin to learn a 'pecking order' and how we align ourselves can be key to how we live our lives going forward. It should not matter who we take to the dance, the key is we all want to 'shake our groove thing' without boundaries or judgement. Thinking back to those dances the truth is the guys hung out together and most of the girls hung out together too. Most times the guys spent the night sitting on the bleachers. So why not have a 'come as you are' dance and don't set expectations of bringing a date. Be yourself and express who you are openly.

We all seem to wait for the right moment or the special invitation to a party, especially when you know an event is being planned. In our adult years we play the same game as we did in High School. Although most of us have a life partner it still comes down to who makes the cut. I compare it to a ranking system and those with the most points gets the golden ticket.

In any event we set the stage for how we associate ourselves with others. The strong will survive. Need to step back and think about how we teach our young in these situations. We begin to set the tone or how our society views others and the diversity of who we are every day. Everyone should have the chance to have the spotlight shine on them, at least once. If anything, it makes you feel good and accepted. There is way too much judgement and rejection today and it becomes the root cause of so many unforeseen events.

Have your dancing shoes on because at this dance you won't be sitting down. Express yourself and pick your song that will cause you to shake it all night long.

Chapter 32

When We Think the Right Things Turns Out Wrong

I t's never easy to make decisions, sometimes it is the hardest thing we do. Sometimes it takes days of thinking it through and may require advice from others. Most times we try to do what is best and imagine the outcome of what we finally choose. There are moments of unrest as the most difficult choices seem to keep us up at night. We can never predict the outcome and if we try to plan for the unexpected it certainly would turn out differently. But regardless of our decisions the outcome, good or bad becomes a life lesson. Or at least we should see it that way.

I spend a lot of time thinking my decisions through and I often times make sure no one gets hurt emotionally. No matter how much I try it seems I failed to plan appropriately. For me I never want people to dislike me or think I intentionally hurt them. I do my best and I guess that is all I can do.

Over time we share our failures and successes with family and friends. They give opinions and support us along the way. It's hard to imagine not having influences in our lives. We look up to others as they teach us right from wrong. Sometimes what we think is right appears to someone else as not the best decision.

There have been many moments that we all can say we "bit out tongue," not figuratively. I meant we hold back because striking back with a response or facial gesture will provoke even more hard feelings and emotions. It's easy to do and most times it does not turn out well.

It's like going into a meeting with an agenda that you have thought about over and over again. You made changes to it multiple times and made sure all the key issues were captured. You prepare for questions and you anticipate who will push back and who will be accepting of your plan. Regardless you plan for success.

Never fails because it only takes one person in that meetings to turn it into a disaster. It's always the one person you knew was coming but never planned for the backlash. After countless hours of preparing you're immediately deflated and left trying to recover the damage. You planned for the best and are left juggling the pieces. So you plan, capture the notes and accept the consequences. Because the true measure is your recovery. Proof that what you set out to accomplish will be what is accepted.

Others may think they know everything, but they don't know you.

Chapter 33

Mother's Day

With the start of Spring comes the celebration of Mother's Day. It makes sense celebrating our Mothers as the Earth begins to give birth to another season. The trees begin to show life and the ground opens up with new life. We prepare our homes with bright flowers and plantings that welcome Summer. Mother Earth is alive with life.

For those of us who reflect on our mothers who are no longer walking this Earth we begin to reflect on the past, remembering our mothers and how we celebrated this holiday. This holiday has countless meanings that go beyond a simple gift of a card or the bouquet of flowers we selected at a local florist. We thank our mothers because they brought us into this world and gave us life.

It's not just another holiday that appears on our calendars every May. It's important to really understand the meaning and why we respect our mothers and thank them for their accomplishments. Just like the earth coming alive with new growth and the sea of green we observe in the forest, it makes us smile with a sense of new beginnings.

The circle of life is a treasure that most of us don't appreciate. We don't take time to observe nor do we reflect on its meaning. Every year we anticipate the Spring as we hold on hope for the last touch of Winter and that last snow fall which blankets the ground.

In early Spring we watch as the tulips poked through the soil and breath in the warmth of the sun. Slowly they make their way. It never fails that as they struggle to come alive nature tends to give them a last blast of cold, only to slow the process down a bit. It is a test of endurance and most time nature seems to pull through and become stronger. Maybe it's the drive within to present itself so we can enjoy the beauty that has been hidden for months. The re-birth of nature that unfolds before our eyes. But have you honestly noticed the process and truly appreciated how life begins and grows?

This time a year is perfect to celebrate our birth and coming to life. The celebration of Mother's and the months of preparation they endured until we were born. Like nature and the tulip bulbs, we take nine months to grow. Mother Nature certainly is consistent. So much around us has unique and many meanings that are hidden and should be explored.

So we tend to celebrate Mother's Day with gifts from nature. The simple flower arrangement from the local florist, to the elaborate house plant we notice while browsing in our local nursery. Regardless of the gift you choose to recognize your mother with it was chosen for a reason. The hidden meaning of the life and growth of these plants reminds us how complex and unique we are, and should not be taken for granted.

No tulip is the same, each leaf of a plant is different from the other and every life brought into this World is special no matter how tall or small, fat or thin, male or female. We accept life as it is and appreciate the beauty it brings.

Celebrate every day as if it was the first day you came to life.

Chapter 34

Road Bumps

You can never predict the future, at least that is the saying we all have heard through our lives. But you can anticipate the outcome. Is that the same thing? If I can anticipate how a conversation or an event will end, then maybe I can predict the future. Often times I try to imagine how a decision will play out and in that process I prepare for what the end result will be. Most times I get it right and sometimes my expectation falls short.

It does not matter how hard we try to prevent others from feeling hurt or annoyed about a particular situation or decision, there is always someone who we did not consider and that one's who's feelings are hurt more. I don't think you can ever plan the entire event or outcome to include everyone's feelings, no one has that power and decisions typically don't include that sort of analysis to secure a positive outcome for everyone included.

If you think of a road bump, when you approach it you slow down and cross over it with caution. The reason we do that is to prevent damage to our vehicles. Life is no different. If you approach a road bump quickly and speed across it, the expectations is we may cause damage. Some bumps are larger than others.

I tend to relate life events to my surroundings and search for meanings that help me do what's right. Silly right? Not necessarily.

Think about road signs and detours we take because of roads that are under construction. Signs posted say; "detour ahead", "proceed with caution", "lane shifts." Now you are scratching your head as to how these signs have life meanings.

Here is how I see these signs:

Detour Ahead – In life we have to be prepared to change our focus. Sometimes our opinions are tested and there are instances when our focus has to take a different path. We don't always agree with the route that is presented to us, but we are forced to follow it since our normal route is not readily available.

Proceed with Caution – Sometimes we are tested with how well we do in our journeys. Our decisions are tested and we don't always have support of family and friends. But we move forward because we clearly want to reach our destination. We take our time, observe the path and make sure we get to the end with no damage.

Lane Shifts – Sometimes we have to shift our direction to allow us to pass by with no distractions. It's a short journey bringing us to our destination. Although there are many road blocks we are able to proceed by slightly changing our path. To me this is the ultimate road sign. It's temporary and one that is easy to manage.

No matter how you choose to move forward there are options that will clear your path. Take note of the signs and follow directions. When you go off the path and ignore signs we tend to get lost and struggle to find our way home.

Why do we not like asking for directions when we get lost on our travels? Are we embarrassed, afraid or simply feel the challenge is worth it? Too often we waist time looking for a familiar course or a landmark that helps us navigate our way back on course. Sometimes that is an easy task but other times we are simply lost.

Most of us don't like asking for help and feel we will burden others. At some point we have all needed a hand and certainly look toward those who we feel more comfortable with to assist. It's not failure and we need to do it more often. Being alone is hard and feeling as if you have no one to support you is more difficult.

Although there were bumps in the road I seemed to smooth those out so my journey was easier. I paved the way to my happiness and feelings of security.

Chapter 35

Mistakes Happen

We are not programmed to be perfect, it's not normal. Mistakes happen and we learn to move on, forgive and forget. Usually the person making the loudest noise is guiltier of a wrong doing. They make noise to move the pressure away, it's the game of life we all play. Many moving parts. Sometimes when you try your best to defuse a situation it always tends to come back at you. I have learned that over and over. At this point my theory is "less is best". Why do we have to share our personal business with everyone? Should be an "as need to know" basis.

It's never easy for anyone to admit to their mistakes and we tend to become defensive as a means of protecting our dignity. Listen, I have made many mistakes along the way and surely will make a lot more in my lifetime. To be honest I have learned from all of them. I am human.

I often explain to customers that errors were caused by "human intervention", and they continue to push for explanations as to "why"? and "what will you do to prevent future mistakes"? When I hear those questions I chuckle to myself. My immediate response would be; "did you ever make a mistake?" Of course to guarantee it will never happen again is absurd. The most disappointing aspect of these questions is that they come from intelligent people who manage people. Do you see the connection?

It difficult to have everyone on the same page and move forward after a mistake impacts them. If you dive deep inside and really think it through there are reasons which lead up to the mistake. Sure some are more severe and cannot be reversed but those are one's which we have to reflect and learn.

Our World being filled with so much hatred and police who make decisions that are life threatening, it's time we slow down and think. We are impacting lives. Even our own Political Representatives are making decisions that take lifetimes to change.

I don't know what the alternatives are but just simply listening to others before decisions are made can certainly help. Our lives depend on so many others and we look for guidance from those who have the most experience. In my job I don't always make the best choices and sometimes I have to re-think my response, however I tend to express how I feel and take our business and employees into consideration.

As much as we try not to judge and find fault in others, we do. No matter how often we do stupid things or make remarks that offend others, we can never make promises that it won't happen again. Sometimes we open our mouths without thinking what the true impact of our words will be. You hear often times that someone has a "sharp tongue" or "they have no filter."

My grandmother's favorite word was "shit." When we were young it was funny to hear her use that word in many forms. Sometimes it was a simple; "oh shit!" That said it all. Often times she would express that "they are full of shit." Whichever phrase she used it was never meant in a harsh tone. Was it bad that she taught her parakeet how to say "shit?" Actually it was pretty funny.

So as hard as we try there will always come a time that we sit back and regret the actions we took or a situation we were in. Never easy to accept that mistakes happen and we do our best at repairing the outcome. That sometimes means making promises that could lead us down a path which opens ourselves up for further mistakes. But we take the challenge and move on.

Don't be afraid of your mistakes, embrace them and plan your recovery with meaningful actions. Remember; accept it, repair it and ask for forgiveness.

Chapter 36

It's Reality

In my position I often have job openings and conduct countless interviews to identify the best candidate for a job. Sometimes the process takes weeks and there are times when you meet the perfect candidate day one. Usually does not happen that easy but eventually you know who is the best person for the job.

Recently we held a two-day event and interviewed multiple candidates back to back. The event was well organized and the candidates we spoke to were pre-screened based on their qualifications. These positions are entry level but certainly hold an opportunity for someone to get a foot in the door. We pride ourselves on motivating our staff to advance their careers and move up in the organization. Usually I tell candidates that I would not be doing my job if I don't see them succeed. I want to see my employees progress.

As the two-day event went on we interviewed a variety of candidates. Some had experience others applied knowing they would have a chance to learn. I enjoy meeting candidates and hearing their path and asking how they got to this table today. Most times I don't ask the typical interview questions, to me that is boring and routine. My approach is a conversation about 'you.'

One candidate told us that he worked in a lab and injected rats and mice with cocaine. His research was to observe how the rodents reacted to coming down off their high. I gave him a lot of credit for doing that job as he explained it was him and the rodents in a room. I guess he was not job shadowing anyone. So after many questions his decision was to change the direction of his career and pursue opportunities in business. Lucky for us because I ended up hiring him. Bad for the rodents I guess.

Next on our itinerary was a gentleman who worked in the healthcare business and was seeking opportunity within our organization. At least that is what he told our recruiter so he seemed to be a good fit. His appointment was for 2:00pm. As it got closer to the time one of my colleagues decided to walk down into our lobby and see if he was waiting for us. I began checking emails as I waited for her return with our candidate.

When I looked up the candidate was standing in the door. I hesitated for a moment but stood up and shook the young man's hand. What I did not expect is this young man was more comfortable in his appearance as a woman. He was professionally dressed in a beautiful suit with matching heels. At that moment I got it. *"Diversity."* I was living the definition, not only as a gay man but now I was accepting the fact that this young person had the confidence to be who he felt comfortable with. It takes a long time to be confident of who you are and if you choose to express yourself differently we tend to hide because of others.

After the interview I turned to the other managers and recruiter in the room to express my feelings. My concern was not about if this person could do the job it was how would others treat him. I was afraid for him. People are hurtful.

I have always heard you look beyond the makeup and the image someone portrays when then are out in public. Sure we tend to touch up our blemishes and fix our hair in the most perfect way, because that is the image we want others to see. But behind all the face creams and hair gel is a person just asking to be accepted. This young man is trying to fit into a World that is not always forgiving.

As I escorted him to the lobby and thanked him for coming in for our interview I realized how important it is to accept everyone for who they are.

Chapter 37

Standing Alone

At some point we find ourselves standing alone in line reflecting on what brought us here. We tend to look around and observe our surroundings and begin to analyze who shares this path. No matter the time it takes to reach the end, we utilize this moment to dig into our inner soul and search for the inner meaning of our existence. It's in these moments we find ourselves reflecting back on the past and planning for the future.

Many people brag about their alone time and speak of how inspired they become when they can sit in silence or walk into their homes and know no one is there. Some how many find that time relaxing. I applaud anyone who can treasure being alone. I of course cannot. Sure I like to have moments to sit alone and think, reflect and plan. But truly being alone weighs heavy on my mind, body and soul.

I remember a time in my life when I was at my lowest. I struggled to feel accepted and I was out of work. My day consisted of logging into my computer and completing on-line applications for jobs I felt qualified for. Each day seemed to weigh heavier and heavier on my shoulders. I watched out the front door as my neighbors left home for work each morning, they had a purpose. Some mornings I wanted to sob into my coffee cup but I had to keep my head up and move on. This new reality was my job. I was dedicated and knew it all would work out. I had to stick with it.

I hated the thought of coming home to an empty house. My home was where I chose to hide and only look out at the World through the front window.

The support of my partner, family and friends helped me. I had people on my side who would not let me fail. As they say; "life throws you lemons, make lemonade." Hell, I was about to open up a lemonade stand on the corner if it was going to help.

Why does this have meaning? My point is we are never alone and should always feel we have support of others. It's what we make of it. If we allow ourselves to be held up in our homes without human interaction, then it's a choice we make. Once you establish your goal and begin to share your journey others tend to follow.

Even if you are the most comfortable in your own skin and never had feelings of being alone, you need to look out for others who appear to need help. Not easy to identify those individuals but look around, listen and observe your community of friends and family. So many people hide behind their walls until someone lends a hand or provides a clear path to climb over what blocks them out.

Standing alone does not mean you have to be alone.

Chapter 38

Around the Table

We can accomplish so much sitting around the table and sharing ideas and thoughts. Tears have been shed over bowels of nacho's and chips and laughter has been provoked with a scoop of ice cream and hot fudge. Does not matter what you choose to serve. We all come together for a cause and share stories. I prefer a round table. What about you? Or does it matter? No matter the shape of your table it's use is more important.

Whether you eat every meal at the table or only use the dining room for special occasions we tend to gather without a set agenda. Everyone is welcome.

As we prepare to gather around the table and prepare for our guest we spend time making the table a centerpiece for our event. We look for the perfect table cloth and place mats; we even get creative with how we put the napkins at each place setting. In the center of the table will be candles, flowers or a creative piece that took us hours to put together. Most times we give a last minute shine to our silverware.

We do all this preparation because we want to make a good impression. Everyone likes a compliment and we want everyone to know how hard we worked to make the event special.

PAUL R. BECKER

If you think back in time, there was a table in most memorable events in history. The Last Supper, Knights of the Round Table, Thanksgiving when the Pilgrims came to America. There are so many to list and you really don't have to think hard about it.

But in any of these situations people came together.

Funny how a piece of furniture holds a special room in our homes. In our recent home search, we came across many homes that used this space for other things. Some used it for a home theatre, others made this room into a play space for their kids.

When we plan a Wedding it becomes a chore to plan out the seating. Countless hours deciding who occupies a chair at the table for 10/12 or less. We think of each person and the personalities they will bring to that gathering. Many changes are made until we feel confident everyone will have a good time. We seem to always have that one table which poses a challenge. Funny how we do our best to ensure everyone is comfortable.

As our guests line up to get their table assignments they immediately begin to evaluate and research who is sitting with whom. Sort of a game that is played. The closest friends or family immediately locate their table number and place a personal article at their seat to claim their spot. We select who will sit next to us and certainly discuss the remaining occupants until each arrives. Why is this an orchestrated process? Why do we care so much? It should be about the couple who we are celebrating.

In the past I have gone to Weddings as a single but with members of my family. There were moments of questioning as I sat apart from my immediately family but at the end of the day it really did not matter. Most of the night after dinner no one stays at their seats.

This table, made of wood and metal has a way of causing many emotions. It's like the game of musical chairs. We juggle around the wood form to claim our spot. The position we choose gives us a sense of comfort. Whether we look towards a window or the dance floor, our place is key.

Although out of our comfort zone we should put table numbers in a hat and let everyone pick their location, no pre planning and no hardships of who gets along better than another. Have our guest randomly pick the location they have to sit at and welcome new conversations. Welcome someone who they have never met before. It may even get people to talk about the experience. Surely would enforce the mixture of all personality types and backgrounds.

We do the same in our homes. Most times we direct people to where they should sit.

Step out of your comfort zone, it could bring opportunities that you would have never pursued.

Chapter 39

What Not to Wear

I often wonder what people think sometimes when they get dressed in the morning. When I look around the City as I walk to work from the parking garage I am amazed, shocked and on the rare occasion impressed. I get most businesses are 'corporate casual' now and the days of a suit and tie are behind us. But what is too much?

The latest trend of yoga pants with an oversized shirt appears to be the new trend. Those pants come in many colors, patterns and sizes. For men I see a lot of untucked shirts with jeans or khaki pants that have not seen an iron since they were purchased.

It's okay to be casual and if you feel comfortable wearing those outfits then so be it.

For me I have always interpreted 'business casual' as a shirt with a collar and pants that have been to the dry cleaners or have been met with a hot iron. Shoes and belt match and I rarely would wear sneakers on Friday's. Actually on a few Fridays I did go out on a limb and wore jeans. I think my staff were left speechless and in shock.

I don't have an opinion either way but I do think we have gotten too casual. When we walk into the door of our employer we are an image that others on the outside see. We represent that company and our appearances should invoke conversation about what we do. If you are in a supervisor or manager role there should be rules. My opinion of course.

Feeling good about how you look is a motivation. We love when others compliment us on how nice we look. I believe that same motivation is what drives us to do well at our jobs. Those who tend to take a more casual approach may not be as driven to succeed.

That holds true to our personal grooming as well.

Most of us want to be taken seriously and strive to be successful. We have dreams and goals, some reachable and others are simply dreams that make us smile.

As I look around I tend to imagine the backgrounds of the individuals who walk around me. I'm not judging their appearance because they are comfortable and they certainly should be. But I wonder what drives them.

When our parents and grandparents were young the style was much more conservative. I remember the first time I flew on a plane with my dad, I had to wear a tie. Which was the norm for me even in grade school. Making an impression was important and we did not worry about being overdressed to provoke conversation of our differences.

What has changed? Why has our society changed? What is the norm?

I believe we have set rules and over time others push the boundaries and in doing so we begin to accept more and more. Or maybe does it just become that we are all too busy to notice? I do think we need to strengthen the rules, it's time to revisit. Maybe because we have become so casual that our society feels that rules don't matter.

Just like dressing up for a special occasion and the feeling of self-worth, we should apply that sense of style daily. It gives us recognition and others will notice you.

The art of style should live in all of us. The feeling of self-worth is an attitude of pride that does not have to break our bank accounts.

You own it!

Chapter 40

Silence is Defining

I always look forward to the Summer months and enjoy sitting out in our courtyard at home. I listen to the birds and the sounds that fill the air on a clear sunny morning. The occasional train in the distance or the car horn that goes off. The sound of a lawn mower humming across a lawn. In our courtyard we have a fountain which is soothing to hear as the water runs down each lever of the vessel. Of course that one bird who thinks it's fun to splash around in it making the water spill over. Would not change that for anything. Actually brings a smile to my face.

I often times drift away in my thoughts and look at the blue sky and watch as a plane passes over thinking of the journey those passengers are taking. Often times wondering where will they eventually land. Once in a while a neighbor walks past as they take their dog on their morning walk. Usually we exchange a "good morning" and go on with our days.

There is a sound of Summer that I miss and it seems to have gone away. In the background the murmur of children playing is no longer. I remember hearing the laughter as kid's road their bikes through neighbors and an occasions scream when someone missed the ball. Those days of kick ball and hop scotch seem a distant memory.

Growing up we used chalk to map out our hop scotch court in the street. The neighbor kids would gather and form a line as we tossed the flat stone onto the court and hopped across the numbers. Eventually the court would be washed away by the rain. But again it would be drawn and another game would take place.

Chalk was used to make bases forming a triangle for the next game of kick ball. On occasion we would have to move to the road side in order to let a neighbor pass by in their car. The kick ball team would wave as the driver encouraged us to "kick a home run."

Unfortunately, those sounds are gone in most neighborhoods, the welcoming murmur of people enjoying a picture perfect day of taking in fresh air. What happened?

Our lives have become focused on TV and games that involve acts of violence. It's about how many points we can accumulate by "taking out the bad guys," or "killing the intruder." Imaginations have been replaced with a hand held device that toggles your way through each episode of the video game. How sad.

The next time you sit outside just listen. Take in the moment and think back to when we could hear voices of happiness. I guarantee you will struggle to hear those sounds.

My grandparents lived in a close community outside the City of Pittsburgh. The homes were close together and parking was limited to on street, very few homes had a garage. Every Sunday we came together for dinner and usually ended up outside in the back yard. My grandfather would show us his garden and brag about this year's tomato crop. If you were quick and could get out to the porch first after dinner the wooden porch swing was yours. It sat three comfortably and you could swing back and forth letting the fresh air hit your face. After dishes were done it was time for banana pop-cycles, or fudge-cycles whichever grandma had in the freezer. Usually that meant the family would take a walk to main street and admire the windows of the local stores.

Thinking back, if we could only sing together we may have become the *Becker Von-Traps*.

But we laughed together as we moved through the streets and would talk to neighbors, wishing them a "happy Sunday."

When I listen now in the distance I hear the tune of wind chimes as the breeze passes over them. I don't hear voices or laughter but I reflect on how life was. I can hold onto those memories forever and cherish them for a lifetime.

I can only speak in silence to those we have lost, but I feel strongly they hear me. Close your eyes and listen hard. We need a little noise!

Chapter 41

The Conversation

One of my challenges is the art of small talk in certain situations. I struggle to initiate a conversation and most times sit and wait until someone else take the lead. In some ways I may be a bit shy or insecure. Most times this is when I am meeting someone for the first time. Obviously more comfortable with friends whom I have known a long time. It may be common for most people but finding the right words is hard. I never want to come across unwilling to engage with others so I normally smile and listen closely until the moment comes to interject an opinion or simply nod in agreement.

Recently went to lunch with two close friends. We went to a local restaurant and sat in a booth facing out into the main dining area. It was a private setting and we could easily talk because the booth was in the shape of a half moon. I sat in the middle. We of course placed our drink order, I had a mojito.

Our conversation started the moment we sat down and continued as we ate. We covered all sorts of topics and laughed together. It was fun catching up and at no point did anyone struggle to find a word. We talked about how we grew up, our parents, family and friends along the way. We shared our good news and listened closely when we talked about our personal lives. That's what friends do.

At no point did anyone "check in" on Facebook or capture a selfie when our food was delivered to the table. Our lunch together was 'our' time. The only time we reached for a cell phone was to share pictures. One of the best lunches I have had with friends in a long time.

We shared stories about our relationships. It is rewarding to have a comfort level with friends who honestly care and not judge. At times we may not agree with each other but at least we are free to express our opinions.

Conversations are not always easy; the topics may not be what your audience wants to hear or expect to be a part of. Either way if you orchestrate them the right way they can offer support or suggestions that will result in a positive outcome.

Remembering back, I struggled with the first time I told anyone I was gay. It was the hardest thing I had to do. I had the biggest lump in my throat and I only imagined the worst outcome. My choice to have this discussion was face to face and certainly not one I wanted to have over the phone.

After we finished dinner we walked around the town of Rehoboth Beach. I was with my cousin Debbie. In my mind and after endless practices I knew what I wanted to say. At least my mind knew but how I would translate to my mouth would be the trick. We went back to the Bed and Breakfast where we were staying and sat in the wicker chairs, the evening was perfect. Nice breeze from the Atlantic Ocean and we were alone on the porch. I remember taking a deep breath and starting to talk. It was a couple years after my divorce and I was getting more comfortable with who I was. As I explained to Debbie she at no point judged me or showed signs of dissatisfaction with who I am. Once my speech was done she simply thanked me for being honest and gave me a hug. I remember her saying; "I love you no matter what." Seems to be the standard answer, but one that is accepted. That simple sentence holds so much value. We don't need a speech about how we should live our lives, we just need to feel loved.

The lump in my throat passed but my eyes filled with tears. Holding those back I was immediately relieved. I guess I could never imagine anyone being told that they were not accepted. What a crushing blow that would be.

In the news recently I heard about a young man who died, he was gay. His family did not approve of his lifestyle and because of that they would not claim his body nor pay for a funeral. This young man had a network of friends who pitched in and were able to raise money in order to bury him with a proper service. How could parents be so cruel?

I cannot imagine the conversation this young man had with his parents and the ignorance his family portrayed. This young man was left to be an orphan in life.

Don't walk away from a conversation with bad feeling. If anything shake hands, hug or a smile.

Chapter 42

True Colors

There is one song that can bring tears to my eyes as I listen to the words over and over. The song has so much meaning and it applies to our world today.

"Show me a smile then don't be unhappy, can't remember when I last saw you laughing. If this World makes you crazy and you've taken all you can bear, you can call me up because you know I'll be there".

We often hear that people show their true colors in certain situations. What does that really mean? True colors and personalities go hand in hand. When we think we know someone and anticipate their reaction is when things turn in another direction.

Our "true colors" should never be a guessing game, we should wear them proud. Do we know our colors and is that why we have our favorites? What does that say about us? Many colors reflect our moods and there are some which provoke us to feel angry, usually dark colors. Bright colors fill us with joy and make us feel welcome.

I often think we surround ourselves with the colors we like most, and that applies to people we know. Our homes are painted with colors that make us happy and we tend to accent walls to express our inner feelings. Why not pick the people we most like by the color they represent? It may be true and something most of us would never think about. It would be interesting to ask your friends what their favorite color is and I would imagine based on their personality it is a color we would like.

But true colors apply to personalities too. Not just the expression of our likes or dislikes. If you dig into the color you associate with it does have a lot of meaning. One of my most favorite colors is blue. Blue is a color that suggests peace. It's the color of the calm sea and the clear sky, both of which are linked to inner serenity, calm and clarity. Blue was also shown to slow heart rate and breathing, so it can be a good color to aid in meditation or relaxation. Not sure how many 'blue' friends I have but I would bet there are a few.

So much of what surrounds us has been chosen by its inner most meaning.

The song certainly applies to how we live our lives and the need to recognize those who are not as fortunate or continue to struggle identifying their color. It's like the open box of crayons, so many to choose from but we don't know which to start with. As a child I loved to color and would spend time using a black crayon first to outline the picture I was coloring in the book. The dark lines gave me a barrier so I knew that I would stay within the lines. But the next step to decide the color I would use first sometimes took time to determine. I had to think about the end result and how I wanted that picture to appear. It really did not matter what I decided because the image I was coloring was my creation. I had control.

If you think about those simple decisions and the thought process, we wanted to create an end result that showed creativity and would finally find its place on the refrigerator. From the color of a character's hair on the page to the green grass in the background we took time to select each crayon.

Seems as though we accept life in a similar way. Our box of crayons is full of color and variety and how we decide to illustrate what makes us the happiest is our decisions.

Chapter 43

Life's a Bitch

How many times have you heard that phrase in your lifetime? Although; is it really? I guess it's what you make of it. We are in the driver seat and how we choose to live it depends on our definition.

As we get older and certainly wiser we begin to figure out who the key players are. We also start thinking of our future and who will be left to look out for us some day. Not having children, you hope that a niece, nephew will take on that responsibility. I tell Chris, Emily, Jessica and Blaire that "my shit" is "their shit" some-day. Actually we joke about putting 'post-it' notes on any items they truly want. Maybe a bit morbid right?

So we look back and recap our lives and some of us create a bucket list. We start writing down places we want to see or those once in a lifetime of opportunities we always wanted to try. On my bucket list I have a few destinations I want to see. One is Switzerland and the other is Vegas baby.

All in all, up to this point I have done okay. Sure we dream of more money, the big house on the beach and the garage full of expensive cars. Not reality but nice to imagine how I would spend my Power Ball winnings. Oh wait; "you have to play to win".

My life surely is not a "bitch" and I feel honored to be living it. It would be hard to imagine that I was never given this opportunity, my parents did well. I write a lot about how things were and the changes that have taken place over time. Many of us will never know how things used to be and will live in a World that will continue to change.

Lives are fragile and don't come with instructions or labels to alert us that we can break if not handled properly. Those are feelings and the hidden ingredients we don't have the luxury to know. Respect is what we all deserve and that word should be under; 'handle with care'.

Your life is what you make of it. Be proud to live it and hold yourself accountable for the outcome. Don't blame others because of failures, fix it and continue on. Pass on what you know, put 'post-it' notes on those keepsakes and feel honored that what you have earned will give others an opportunity.

Chapter 44

Toxic

At some point we begin to look at our own network and begin the task of identifying those who we call friends, acquaintances and family. We tend to first look at who we hear from most or those who we "like" their posts more than others. For some this task is more difficult to do and others find it refreshing, like cleaning the house on a Spring morning with the windows open.

The ones we tend to "unfriend" have at some point proved to be a disappoint to us in one way or another. The others we identify as toxic. Those people we push away because their influence in our lives has a negative impact.

Why do we go through this process multiple times throughout our lives? It starts at a young age and continues through our adulthood.

As we learn our place in this World is important to surround yourself with people who are equally prepared to support your journey. It's how we survive and how we determine our direction.

If you truly think about who you have in your mix of friends those individuals should be your immediate "go to" people. This group will be honest and offer support in times of need and will lift you when you fall. Anyone identified as a "friend" will be around for a long time. Cherish this group forever and be cautious when adding new members.

Acquaintances are people we talk to from now and then. They come around when you have a party only to observe who else is in the room. We don't necessarily reach out to these members consistently but follow their actions just to know they exist. Our acquaintances are not our "go to" people, most we have not seen in a long time. We just keep those people around and certainly don't want to lose their connection.

Our Family is just that. We should put these names at the top of our list and it is easy to identify them. Actually, some friends become your family and that title is earned. Of course we get upset with our family members from time to time and especially those who post nonsense and tend to be the outcast. Hopefully you don't have many of those.

So what's left? From time to time identifying those who are "toxic" is a good exercise. These people at one time fit into one of those categories but over time they have drifted away. Or, this group really does not have your best interest at heart and routinely seem to have something negative to say.

Why do we keep them? It's only a click away. After some time, you don't enjoy reading their post and your anxiety level reaches a point of "blocking them". It's okay to let them go. You own your list. Don't be afraid to clean out those toxic people. Certainly does you no good to keep them around.

I used to worry that I would offend someone or they would talk about me for clicking "unfriend" at some point. Honestly I have come to a point that I need people in my life who I 'want to have in my life'. Those who have made an impression on me, and of course people I truly love as family and friends.

It sounds like I am preparing the roster for the NFL, but my point is to encourage everyone to gain a network of people who are there for you.

Sure, I tend to repeat that over and over and sometimes I don't practice what I preach. Although this time I am.

Understanding respect and living a life where we continually question diversity is teaching me so many life lessons. We fall into the trap of just letting things go or I don't want to make waves or cause hurt feelings. Bottom line is; these individuals who we identify as toxic have at least once or twice hurt you.

Toxic People = *Jealous* **people** *are incredibly* **toxic** *because they have so much internal self-hate that they can't be happy for anyone around them. And typically, their jealousy comes out as judgment, criticism or gossip. According to them, everyone else is awful, uncool or lacking in some way.*

Chapter 45

The Next Generation

We tend to save things that mean the most to us in the hope they will be passed down to the next generation. At least we "hope" someone will keep our memories alive. Although we see value in a pocket watch, a holiday pin our mother's wore on Christmas Day to Church or a letter that was written long ago to a love one. Some of these things could have monetary value but we save them in a drawer or box to hand off to someone who will cherish it forever.

I often speak of my Aunt Colette and the value she added to my life. Over the years she would tell the story about her dining room set that she worked so hard to buy. She worked for Joseph Horne's in Pittsburgh and would purchase one piece of the set at a time. Most often a chair would sit in "lay-away" until she paid the balance. Her story stuck with me a long time. Aunt Colette worked hard to eventually have an entire set, which was proudly displayed in her home. Many fun times in that room and lots of stories were shared at family meals. If only those chairs could talk.

At one point in her life she moved into Assisted Living and our family came together and packed up her belongings as the house was put up for sale. We climbed into the attic and pulled boxes of shoes, purses and holiday decorations one by one. It was fun digging into those boxes and finding those hidden treasures.

We placed things into piles labeled; *Keep, Toss and Donate*. Yellow post-it notes were stuck to the living room wall and those sections started filling up.

As we all took claim to pieces of furniture and many other treasures everyone seemed to have no interest in the dining room set. Not because of its condition, but because no one had room for it. Kyle and I began loading a truck with Goodwill items and made a few trips back and forth until all the small items were left. When it came down to the dining room we halted for a moment before making a final decision. We could not do it. That dining room had to find a home and it was an easy decision that it belong to us. There was no way this set would end up sitting on the floor in a Goodwill shopping center. It had history, it had a story and it meant the world to our aunt.

Regardless if the set fit into our home décor this furniture had to remain in the family for another generation to enjoy. It's not about the type of wood or the whether or not a chair needed repaired. There is certainly a lesson in how this furniture came into our family and what it meant to my aunt as she accomplished a goal to own it. It represents dedication and commitment, hard work and the drive to achieve a goal.

When we welcome family and friends to join us for dinner and sit at this furniture we should share the story and talk about the memories that will last a lifetime. My aunt created a memory when she put the first piece on layaway at Joseph Horne's and I bet she never knew it.

Most of what we take for granted and things that have been handed down to us tend to be objects with no purpose, at least until we understand their story and more important how one simple object can influence our lives.

Be proud to talk about your past and don't be afraid to share failures too. Not always about what we accomplished and everything that positively influenced us. My Aunt may not have always had the money for her next payment on the furniture, so she worked extra hours so she could double up the next time. That is dedication and commitment.

The furniture sits in our home today and will never lose its place. Gladly displayed and polished every weekend we are proud to share how it come to rest. Every holiday the table is decorated with an appropriate centerpiece which only adds value to its appearance. This object without feelings has touched our lives forever.

Chapter 46

The Perfect Image

In our search to be accepted we look at media to help identify our appearance. We spend time paging through magazines and looking at celebrities on various shows who we tend to view as a role model. It becomes our never ending search for the perfect 'me'. Very seldom do you see an average person advertising clothing, or a person with an average face trying to sell cosmetics at the local counter. We paint on an image in the attempt to duplicate what we think looks good on us. This task to look a certain way turns out to be a mistake. We all want to feel good and maintain our looks forever. I am all for it.

What is the perfect image? Or is there one? I don't think anyone can say for sure that someone has the 'look'. Surely we recognize a good looking person and think to ourselves; why is that not me?

Sitting in the local hair salon I am often amazed at how many parents control how their children's hair is cut. They tell the hair stylist exactly the right length and on which side their hair should be parted on. The child sitting in the chair tries to give an opinion but is immediately turned away and the haircut continues as Mom & Dad express their opinions. Surely if a child is unable to make those decisions on their own I see when parents need to speak up. I often see Mom & Dad paging through magazines in the shop giving pointers as to what would look best for their son or daughter.

Maybe the child or young adult needs to have their own opinion on what they want. Surely they have an idea in their mind and want what is best for them. At this age these wonderful young people are looking for their image. At some point we need to allow them to share in the experience.

It's hard finding yourself and the image you want to see looking back at you in the mirror. I at one time colored my hair to cover up the gray. I quickly gave up on that one. Those white hairs were coming fast. So I embrace my new look and decided I had to go with it. What was the alternative? A wig? Shave my head? I don't think so.

Chapter 47

Share The Knowledge

Over time we gather information and keep it stored up in our brains. In a lifetime we should have enough knowledge and experience to teach the World, or a small subset at least. As we learn and observe it becomes apparent that in us we have the ability to influence others. If we put our minds together just think of the opportunities.

So why don't we put our minds together? Some of us believe so strongly in what we think we know that we don't open ourselves up to hear what others have to say. Having an open mind is hard for many, as we get stuck in our ways that we forget others may have experienced similar situations, and may have dealt with them differently. This truly is key to have diversity in all we do.

You often hear; there are no dumb answers or stupid questions. Are there?

Everyone is encouraged to speak their minds and offer ideas or suggestions in a meeting environment. Most times the facilitator calls on someone to speak up or offer their thoughts to the subject at hand. As we listen to what this individual says you can anticipate eyes rolling or the gentle whisper as others around the table find it time to offer their opinions. So the person speaking is left to feel as if what they said was not appropriate. Certainly not the impression we want to make but it does suggest it.

Many personalities and experiences sit in this meeting and have invaluable knowledge to share. But not everyone will share what they know or want to express ideas because of the reactions they anticipate. Although we want interaction it's hard to engage everyone. People should never feel embarrassed or afraid. We don't do well accepting opinions of others and most who don't have a comfort level to speak often times hold the key to our discussions.

What we have to change in these situations is rules, set expectations and give our audience a voice. I have been in meetings where everyone is given a post-it note to write their ideas down and remain anonymous, and I often think how sad that is. It does not matter what you say because the idea you want to share is one that you believe in strongly. Your vision.

It's unfortunate that we can only dream of our vision as selling it to others is hard. Even though we feel strongly about our idea for change it takes facts and examples to prove it will work. Recently I joined a new department at work. I see a lot of change, I observe many situations that I would approach differently and I walk a fine line too. Why is that? Sometimes I hold back because "I'm the new guy", other times I sense that things have been this way for a long time and it would take an act of God to change.

I keep pressing forward and take note of what I would do differently and store that knowledge for another time, the right time, when it is appropriate to share. My style of management is one of communication and sharing ideas. I want to hear what others have to say and I expect people who work for me to try new things. As in business and our personal lives we can always use change and finding a new way of doing things. What was does not always means it is the best way.

Chapter 48

Faces

When you look in the mirror the image of the person looking back is you. In a crowd that same image is unrecognizable by many. We become another face in the crowd. The image we portray is how we want others to see us. Often enough we struggle with what our reflections look like. That extra wrinkle around our eyes, or the skin blemish that was not there yesterday. We wash our face hoping that after we dry off there will be an improvement. It's not that simple sometimes.

The next time you stand in front of the mirror look harder, study the reflection and simply appreciate the gift your parents gave you. Without them the reflection looking back would be blank. Study the features you see in your parents, siblings and relatives, they are all there. I have my mother's lips and mouth, my father's nose and my image resembles my Uncle John, who was my mother's brother. For many years growing up people asked if I was his son.

But most important is the look deep into your eyes. They lead the path to all you have experienced. When I shave in the morning I often stop and stare at the man I have become. I see in my mind the images of the boy who previously looked in the mirror and dreamt of adulthood. There are moments I stop and think of each path I took that lead me here today. Then I wonder what image do others see when they look at me.

Are others as critical of me in the same manner I am when I recognize my imperfections?

My reflection is what others know of me, but don't necessarily have an idea of who I am and were I have been. In crowds we tend to look at others in passing with a quick smile or a brief stare. Could you ever capture the expressions that one face can make? Our reflections hold many emotions.

The next time you stand in front of the mirror look at the many expressions we make. Men tend to move their mouth to allow for that close shave. We tilt our heads in an effort to make sure every inch is clean and smooth. Women close their eyes when applying eye makeup or squeeze their lips together when putting on lipstick. Our faces have their own routine.

Sometimes that mirror is hard on us, our faces reveal hard times. We see the battle wounds and try with soap and water to wash them away. The pressure we allow ourselves to feel weighs heavily no matter what circumstances brought you to this point. That old wash cloth hanging next to the sink is not going to remove those years of hurt. The best creams and lotions won't take away the stress we endure in our lifetime.

Confidence in ourselves, happiness in our hearts and the feeling of being loved will transition our face to show proudly in a crowd.

Chapter 49

Commitment

No matter the type of relationship you are in, and it certainly does not matter as long as you are happy and confident that how you choose to live works for you and your partner. Relationships take commitment and require a lot of communication. Good or bad you need to talk and keep an open mind. It's also about respect.

Our lives are so busy these days and most couples work a full time job. Together they run a household and bring a family together. The expectations are set then a couple commits to live their lives together. Family comes in many forms but the concept of how the family works is transparent.

Couples work as a team and most hold strong for a lifetime. Surely any relationship is going to have challenges but the 'team' knows how to get through those rough times and look toward a smooth road ahead.

Regardless if we choose a traditional ceremony to states the vows of marriage or decide to create our own moments, those words we convey to each other has a lot of meaning. In our relationship we decided early on to write letters to one another and exchange rings. We don't have a 'legal' marriage but we committed to a long lasting relationship. Now that our union is recognized our desire is to formally have a ceremony.

Nothing bid, nothing formal, just a simple act of letting our friends and family know we are a couple.

Besides a relationship we commit to our careers, our communities and a bond to those we keep close in our lives. Friends will always stand behind each other and will stand with us in difficult times. Of course family is there for the long hall.

It's when we notice that our commitments to others tend to be 'one sided' is when we begin to question when the time comes to consider the relationship over. We never want to say goodbye to people who have been in our lives but there are times that letting go is the best alternative. Why should we hurt?

Taking a moment to step back from any situation and understanding where and when it went badly helps to secure how you proceed going forward. We learn so much from our mistakes and if we truly want to move on and be a better person you have to admit your wrongs. All of us deserves happiness.

In the gay community having a long term relationship is rare. It's difficult at best. I could never imagine at this point in my life being back out on the dating scene. I believe one of the biggest struggles is due to the fact we struggle enough to be accepted in the World so the pressure of a relationship requires dedication.

Some communities have accepted us easier than others. We can live among families and enjoy the benefits of the 'American Dream'. That's the way it should be.

It's funny when you think about it because you hear all the time; 'thank goodness the gays moved in'. We have a way to 'pretty up' the eye sore of the neighborhood. If you think of neighborhoods that struggled to survive and the gay community moved in they begin to thrive and change.

Not only do we have our commitment to one another but we have commitment to the value of family. We love the same, laugh out loud and hurt no differently than any straight couple. The boundaries of 'straight' or 'gay' need to be categorized as 'a couple'. Our neighbors introduce us by name, not by our sexuality.

Commitment is about support and dedication as a couple and is not defined by who we choose to love.

Chapter 50

Strength

The measure of strength can come in many forms. Not just a physical measure of how many pounds someone can lift during their workout. Also the measure of strength is compared to how much pressure a plastic bag can take before it breaks. No matter what we are trying to define it is clear the definition has multiple meanings.

How do we measure our strength to handle life events? There is only so much a person can handle before life crashes around them. Everyone has their own level and can only handle a certain amount.

Strength is also an emotional measure that defines us. When we awake every morning it requires strength to begin our day. We tend to set the expectation of the day and in our minds we prepare ourselves to what is ahead. Our strength to take on a new day is the drive that allows us to put both feet on the floor and take that first breath of a new day.

There are many who struggle to accept a new day and find it more challenging to put both feet on the floor. The simple steps we take every morning to greet the fresh aroma of the coffee brewing is a challenge some struggle to achieve. Bed becomes a secure place that protects them from the world. Those are the people we need to lend a hand to. They are hidden and live behind walls that many never get to see over.

We have all had those times when our secure space is the bed we sleep in. It takes time to find the right path that leads us out into a World that is waiting to greet us. Of course we will stumble and trip but once our feet are grounded and secure we can continue down the path.

Our inner strength is what gives us the drive to move forward and sometimes that strength needs reminded that it's needed. When we have an inner secret to share it takes all we have to share with others. Our secure place helps us hold those secrets in because we then don't feel like the World should know. Not everything needs to be shared, but if we have something to tell that frees us from that space it's time to let go.

Many of us who held in our sexuality for decades find freedom in lifting that burden from our shoulders. We walk among others with a confidence to live our lives proudly. The strength to feel welcomed in many communities is a rewarding feeling. Many couples and single people should wake up every day knowing the lines of differences have been erased.

Get out of bed every day, walk out the front door and smile. This is the life we live. Support one another and simply welcome those we are not like us into the World.

Don't hide, celebrate every day.

Chapter 51

Goes Around Comes Around

Making the best choices throughout our lives never seems to be the easiest thing. Testing the waters in hopes of finding what we feel is the best choice appears to be the norm. Sometimes a 'drop and run' opens the introduction for immediate feedback and gets more attention. However, we choose to live our lives and communicate is our choice. Remember to be honest, truthful and show respect.

It always seems that one time we don't fully tell the story it some-how comes back to bite us in the ass. Never fails! I can remember times when I told my parents I was going to have a few friends over while they were on vacation, just a few. Well, it turned out to be about 50 people. We had a good time, that's what my parents would have wanted. No matter how hard I made sure the house was clean for their return I would miss one piece of evidence under the china cabinet. Of course it was a party decoration, paper cut out of a fish. That made sense since I had a beach party. In the winter, with a pool of beer in the living room, and beach balls tossed around the house. But, nothing was broken. That should count for something right?

But sometimes choices we make are not as simple as a party decoration appearing under a china closet. There are moments that we reacted to a situation or told a story that was not completely the truth and it came back to us. Did you ever wonder how that works?

No matter how small we think our network is it actually is interwoven with others. Like the old game of 'telephone'. We would tell one person a story and as it went around the room it was amazing how that story grew.

Not everyone fits into a network but are left outside to only imagine what stories are being told. Making sure your audience is listening and understands that accuracy is most important, we set rules. Our past life somehow catches up to us. We can embrace it and applause where we have come or dwell on the wrong road we took that also could lead us to the place we are today.

Honesty is the best policy.

It does not come easy at times because we just want to fit in. So we tell stories or twist the truth a bit only to feel equal to those we trust. However, the tale we tell is the one which will be repeated over and over until someday we finally hear a version of what we told.

Chapter 52

Comfort Zone

At some point we become comfortable with ourselves and begin to live the life we were born to live. It takes years of identifying with who we are and getting a sense of where we best fit. Sometimes it's not as easy as we think, however others naturally feel comfortable.

It's the understanding of our emotional feelings and suppressing those emotions is more difficult. I remember the episode of the Golden Girls when Blanche's Brother announced he was getting married to his boyfriend. Rose of course could not grasp the concept and the girls tried to explain it, I think Dorothy true to form hit Rose over the head with a newspaper. Rose finally understanding that Blanche's Brother was marrying a gay police officer. Back then the acceptance of a gay couple was a struggle for many to grasp.

Not all gay couples choose to marry, some live their lives together with a bond that does not require a license to unite their relationship.

Our comfort zone is also the protective approach we take to remain private in anything we do. Not everything we do requires the world to know. That has always been an amazing aspect of social media. You don't need to share it all.

Sometimes I choose to remain silent, seldom share and keep a lot of me/us private. When I wrote my first book I never told anyone I was doing it. I kept that private and work hard to write my emotions out on a tablet of paper, many at best. It was a time to soul search and dig into my soul to find the exact words to express how I was feeling. I tried to tell my story in simple words but to get a point across. That time was rewarding to me. Huge accomplishment that I am grateful for. As you read I hope I achieved it again.

Regardless of how you choose to share your emotions and expressions of unity and commitment it comes down to choice.

In the episode of the Golden Girls a woman came to the dinner table and wanted to meet Blanche's brother. As he began to introduce his partner Blanche began to yell "fire." She purposely took that moment to avoid this woman from finding out her brother was gay. Surely an approach no one wants to ever live through or experience. But, that was Blanche's comfort zone, she could not accept the introduction.

If anything we should openly accept others for who they are and not what we prefer them to be. Others may have opinions and certainly they are entitled. With so much attention on our community and many who have come out publicly we at this point in time need acceptance.

Break out of your comfort zone and keep an open mind.

Chapter 53

Conclusion

It's difficult to know how you will be treated by others no matter what situation you are in. We should never have to worry or think about the reactions that we may get. Everyone deserves to be accepted in a world of uncertainty. We laugh the same, shed tears when we hurt and celebrate our special moments in similar ways.

My stories are simple but written from the heart. I do my best to express my own feelings and want to share experiences to help others. I know I am not perfect and would never claim to be. I make mistakes and act on poor judgement just as we all do. Unfortunately, that's life. If I could redo all my bad choices I would, but I cannot so I live with the fact I learned a lesson.

What we can do is respect each other and have an open mind and learn to listen. People are unique and everyone has something to offer. Does not matter race, sexual orientation or political party. Our opinions do matter but we need to respect each other for our differences.

Creating a world where we can all live without boundaries and hate seems out of reach. Many before us have done their best to break down walls and unite communities. It is not an easy task and truthfully the responsibility of ownership is with you and me. Simply put it comes down to taking charge.

If you dig into the "root cause" of where we are today, the answer is easy. Each of us contributes to making things right, correcting bad behavior and ensuring we accept anyone who is different. There is no time to point fingers, we have to admit our wrongs and make sure our followers don't repeat bad behavior.

Each of us has to take responsibility for our actions and opinions. Some of us express opinions more than others and most hold everyone accountable for their actions. There are times that we don't have control on people's behaviors, but repeating their behaviors only heightens the negative opinions.

At the end of the day; *You Are Who You Are and I Am Who I Am.*

No one will ever change that. But respect is the key to a future of opportunity. Just be honest and admit your mistakes. We need to promote a World of acceptance and support those who have fear of speaking out.

Listen to the voices of those who look up to you as a Leader. Their opinions matter.

Respect is earned, not handed on a silver platter.

It does not matter which community you live in or support, at the end of the day we all want someone in our lives to love and finish our lives with as we grow old. As long as each of us are happy in the skin we were born into, it should never come with color or sexual orientation.

Printed in the United States
By Bookmasters